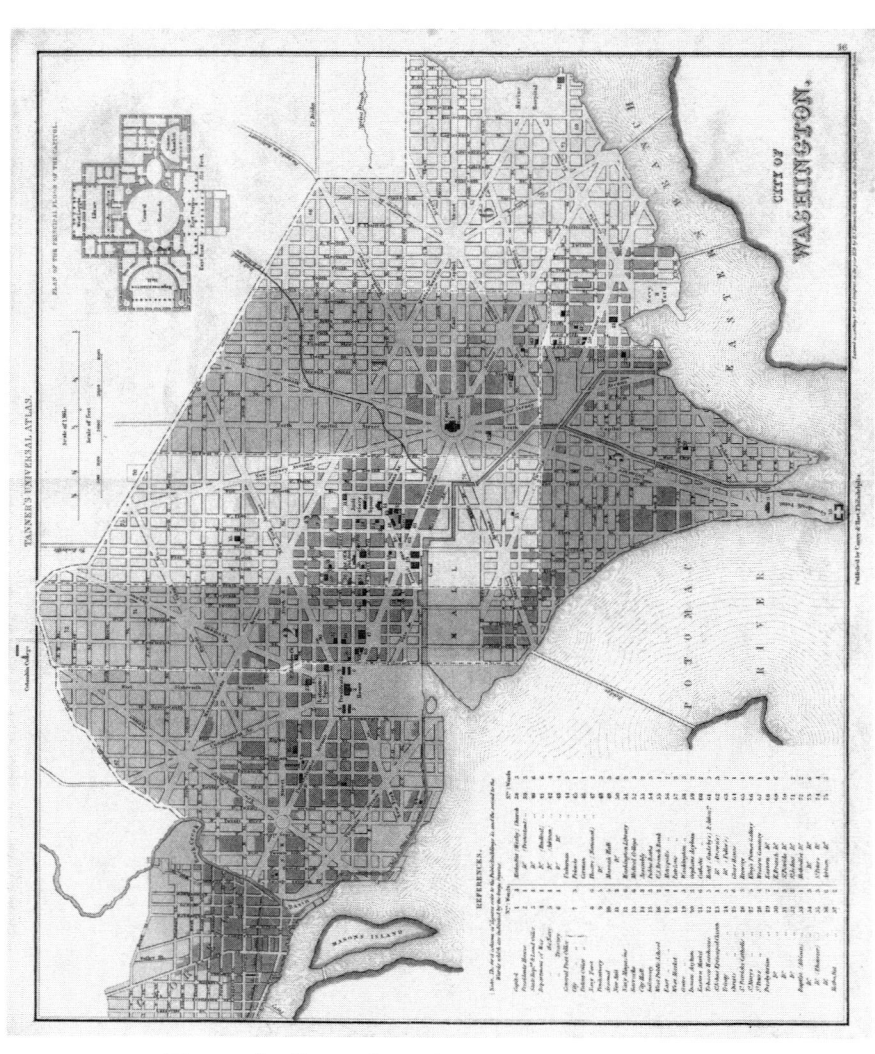

Tanner's *City of Washington* 1836 [PW127]

Maps and Views

of

Washington and District of Columbia

by

P. Lee Phillips, F.R.G.S

Published originally in 1900

Second Edition

Terra Nova Press
G.B. Manasek, Inc.
Norwich, Vermont 05055-1204
1996

Copyright © 1996 by F.J. Manasek. All rights reserved.

ISBN Nº 0-9649000-2-5

First edition: 1900
Second edition: 1996

Introduction to the Second Edition

In preparation for the centenary celebration, P. Lee Phillips created this list of maps and views from the vast collection in the Library of Congress. Now, almost one hundred years later, we still find his list important and useful. Washington, D.C. is, by world standards, still a very young city. As such, a wealth of original documents, plans, surveys and other historical records relating to its early years, and the planning that went into building it, still exist. Nonetheless, the early years of this city have receded from direct human memory and have come to reside solely in the written record. During this time also, contemporary printed maps and views have become scarcer, yet are collected much more widely. There is increasing interest in the earlier periods of our country and much is focussed on the dynamic aspects of our cities.

Phillips' germinal list has long been out of print and not easily available to the collector or dealer. In preparing this second edition we have completely reset the body of the work. In so doing, we were faced with a serious problem. The original text had curious contractions, spellings and capitalization. For example, months of the year were not capitalized and in some cases several variant spellings of a word appeared. We decided to retain these features, and the new text, as much as possible, retains the flavor of the original. In a few instances we corrected the more serious error; in some instances we draw the readers' attention to the original so that it is not assumed to be an error we have committed.

We have added numbers to each entry. These numbers, each with a "PW" (Phillips' Washington) prefix will facilitate referring to this list. We also added the frontispiece.

For a work such as this to have retained its uniqueness and value for nearly a century is remarkable. Its reissue has been long overdue and we are pleased that it is again available readily to the increasingly large group of people interested in this area.

F.J. Manasek
Norwich, VT
1996

| 56TH CONGRESS, | SENATE. | DOCUMENT |
| 1st Session. | | No. 154. |

LIST OF MAPS AND VIEWS

OF

WASHINGTON AND DISTRICT OF COLUMBIA

IN THE

LIBRARY OF CONGRESS

BY

P. LEE PHILLIPS, F. R. G. S.

Superintendent of Maps and Charts

February 7, 1900. – Presented by Mr. McMillan
and ordered to be printed

WASHINGTON
GOVERNMENT PRINTING OFFICE
1900

LETTER OF TRANSMITTAL

The Library of Congress
Washington, February 5, 1900.

SIR: I have the honor to transmit herewith a list of the maps and views of Washington and the District of Columbia from 1782 to 1900, in the Library of Congress. This list has been for some time in process of compilation by the Chief of the Division of Maps and Charts in the library. An examination of it will, I think, show that it represents careful cartographic and bibliographic work.

In connection with the approaching centenary the general interest in the historical development of the city should render this list both pertinent and of value. It is offered to your committee, to be put into print if your decision as to its value and appropriateness shall coincide with ours.

Very respectfully,

Herbert Putnam,
Librarian of Congress.

Hon. JAMES McMILLAN,

Chairman Committtee on the District of Columbia,
United States Senate.

LETTER OF SUBMITTAL.

SIR: I have the honor to submit a report on the maps and views of Washington and the District of Columbia from 1782 to 1900, in the Library of Congress.

As many of the maps and views are found to illustrate some descriptive text in books, the report is not only cartographical but also bibliographical.

The national as well as local interest in all subjects pertaining to the city of Washington, especially in view of the approaching centenary, should make this paper of timely value.

Very respectfully yours,

P. Lee Phillips.

Hon. HERBERT PUTNAM,
Librarian of Congress.

MAPS AND VIEWS OF WASHINGTON AND DISTRICT OF COLUMBIA.

AUTHORS AND DATES
[The dates refer to chronological order in body of the work.]

Alexandria, D. C.
    1798.
    1845.
Allen, Lane & Scott.
    1892.
American magazine of useful and entertaining knowledge.
    1834-1835.
    1837.
American scenery.
    1839.
Anderson.
    1838.
Andrews.
    1834.
Appleton.
    1866.
    1892.
Arlington publishing co.
    1886.
Armytage.
    1863.
Arnold.
    1862.
Arrowsmith.
    1808.
Asch bach.
    1861.
Atlantic magazine.
    1820.
Averill.
    1892.
Baker.
    1793.
Baltimore and Ohio railroad co.
    1853.

Bantz.
    1874.
Barksdall.
    1892.
Bartlett.
    1839.
    1856?
Bartlett & Woodward.
    1863.
Bastert.
    1872.
Bechler.
    1864.
Bell lithographing co.
    1891.
Bennett.
    1834.
Bent.
    1793.
Bernhard (Carl, herzog von Sachsen Wiemar Eisenach).
    1825.
Berry.
    1891.
    1892.
Blanchard.
    1819.
Bliss.
    1867.
Blodget.
    1888.
Bohn.
    1849.
    1854.
    1858.
    1860.
    1861.
    1866.

Maps and Views of District of Columbia

Boschke.
    1857.
    1861.
Boyd.
    1882.
    1884.
Bradford
    1835.
    1838.
Brannan.
    1828.
Brockhaus.
    1895.
Brown.
    1831.
    1834.
    1840?
    1889.
Bruff.
    1889.
Buckingham.
    1841.
Bullfinch.
    1821.
    1828.
Burton.
    1831.
Bussard.
    1830.
Capitol centennial committee.
    1791.
    1814.
    1816.
    1821.
    1830.
    1839.
    1840.
    1841.
    1848.
    1893.
Carey & Lea.
    1822.

Carpenter.
    1870.
Catlin.
    1820.
Century atlas.
    1897.
Chicago chronicle.
    1899.
Christian endeavor convention.
    1896.
Clarke.
    1798.
Clover.
    1834.
Coast and Geodetic survey.
    1862.
    1877-1896.
    1880-1892.
    1892.
Cole.
    1885.
    1886.
    1890.
    1899.
Colles.
    1789.
Colton.
    1856.
    1858.
    1861.
    1862.
    1864.
    1876.
    1878.
    1882.
Commissioners.
    1886.
    1889.
    1894.
    1896.
    1897-99.
    1898.
    1899.

MAPS AND VIEWS OF DISTRICT OF COLUMBIA

Compagnoni.
   1822.
Congressional directory.
   1861.
   1870.
   1877.
   1879.
   1883.
   1886.
   1888.
   1895.
Cook.
   1834.
Corbett.
   1861.
Cowles.
   1862.
Coyle.
   1853.
Cram.
   1899.
Currier & Ives.
   1892.
Darton.
   1896.
Davis.
   1830.
De Krafft.
   1817.
   1822.
   1824.
   1826.
   1828.
Dermott.
   1796.
   1797-98.
Deroy.
   1848.
Desilver.
   1857.
Detournelle.
   1815.
   1816.

Directories. Washington.
   1827.
   1850.
   1853.
   1866.
   1867.
   1868.
   1869.
   1870.
   1882.
Disturnell.
   1837.
Dodge.
   1883.
Donegan.
   1872.
Dougal.
   1887.
Du Bois.
   1892.
Eclectic atlas.
   1881.
Ellicott.
   1792.
   1793?
   1814.
   1815.
   1852.
Elliot.
   1822.
   1827.
Enthoffer.
   1872.
   1873.
Ermer.
   1825.
Evening Star.
   1889.
Ewing.
   1845.
Faehtz.
   1791.
   1874.

MAPS AND VIEWS OF DISTRICT OF COLUMBIA

Fanning.
    1853.
Farley.
    1826.
Fava.
    1890.
Finley.
    1824.
    1889.
Fisher & Co.
    1884.
    1888.
    1890.
    1891.
    1899.
Fitch & Pox.
    1874.
Fontaine.
    1896.
Force.
    1820.
    1822.
    1823.
    1845.
Forsyth.
    1856.
    1868.
    1870.
    1899.
Fort Dearborn publishing co.
    1896.
Fraser.
    1874?
French.
    1854.
Gamble.
    1865.
    1866.
    1870.
    1873.
    1876.
    1878.
    1879.
    1880.
    1882.
    1884.
    1893.
Gerretson, Cox & co.
    1895.
Gedney.
    1885.
    1886.
    1887.
Genesco country.
    1791.
Genesee tract.
    1791.
Geological survey.
    1882.
Geological survey-Continued.
    1893.
    1895.
    1896.
Gilpin.
    1798.
Glenwood cemetery.
    1854?
Goodacre.
    1831.
    1842.
Gothaischer hof-kalender.
    1795.
Graham.
    1853.
    1899.
Gray.
    1873.
    1875.
    1876.
    1882.
    1889.
Green.
    1880.
Greenleaf.
    1792-1801.
Griffith.
    1794.
Haas.
    1840.
Hadfield.
    1793-1811.

MAPS AND VIEWS OF DISTRICT OF COLUMBIA

Haley.
    1861.
Hall.
    1866.
Hall & Elvans.
    1867.
Hallet.
    1792-1794.
    1793-1811.
    1794.
Hamilton.
    1792.
Handy.
    1863.
Hannot.
    1863.
Harrison.
    1827?
    1830.
Harrower.
    1884.
Hart & Von Arx.
    1885.
Hesselbach.
    1862.
Hill.
    1852.
Hill, engraver.
    1792?
Hinman.
    1881.
Hinshelwood.
    1872.
Hinton.
    1831.
    1834.
    1842.
Hoban.
    1793-1811.
Holtzman.
    1885.
Hopkins.
    1877.
    1878.
    1879.
    1887.
    1891.
    1892.
    1893-94.
    1894.
    1896.
Hunt & Eaton.
    1893.
Ingraham.
    1814.
James.
    1814.
Janson.
    1807.
Jarvis.
    1897.
Johnson.
    1862.
    1864.
    1868.
    1883.
    1892.
Jones.
    1802.
    1804.
Keily.
    1850.
    1851.
Keim.
    1888.
Kengla.
    1883.
King.
    1803?
    1803.
    1811.
    1852.
Köllner.
    1848.
Lane.
    1838.

MAPS AND VIEWS OF DISTRICT OF COLUMBIA

Lang.
    1886.
Lanman.
    1858.
    1860.
Latrobe.
    1792-1801.
    1793-1811.
    1803.
    1805.
    1807.
    1807-1817.
    1810.
    1811.
    1815.
    1817.
    1828.
League of American wheelmen.
    1897.
L'Enfant.
    1791.
Lizars.
    1819.
Lukesh.
    1894.
    1894-95.
    1895.
M'Clelland.
    1846.
    1850.
    1854.
    1855.
    1858.
Mackenzie.
    1818.
    1819.
Malte-Brun.
    1834.
Marceau.
    1822.
Marr.
    1887.
Martenet.
    1873.
    1884.
    1885.

Martin.
    1835.
Massachusetts magazine.
    1792.
Matthews-Northrup co.
    1893.
    1898.
Maverick.
    1791.
Meyer
    1845.
Meyers.
    1897.
Middle states of North America.
    1791.
Mills.
    1847.
Milne.
    1882.
Mitchell.
    1849.
    1851.
    1853.
    1865.
    1866.
    1867.
    1870.
    1873.
    1876.
    1878.
    1879.
    1880.
    1882.
    1884.
    1893.
Monk.
    1861.
Moore.
    1802.
    1804.
Morrison.
    1855.
    1868.
    1874.

Maps and Views of District of Columbia

Morrison Continued.
    1876.
    1884.
    1885.
    1888.
Morse.
    1794.
Munger.
    1814.
National calendar.
    1820.
    1822.
    1823.
Neagle.
    1834.
Newby & Co.
    1887.
New York magazine.
    1792.
Norris (The) Peters co.
    1890.
    1894.
    1896.
    1899.
North American bibliographical institution.
    1840?
Ogden.
    1876.
Our globe.
    1840?
Parsons.
    1880.
    1890.
Phelps.
    1853.
Philadelphia public ledger.
    1899.
Philp.
    1861.
Porter.
    1886.
Post office department.
    1881.

Potomac river.
    1862.
    1877-1896.
    1882.
    1887.
Pratt.
    1791.
Priggs.
    1793.
Rand, McNally & co.
    1877.
    1880.
    1881.
    1884.
    1892.
    1893.
    1894.
    1895.
    1896.
    1897.
    1898.
    1899.
Raymond.
    1889.
Reid.
    1795?
Reid, Wayland & Smith.
    1795.
Ritchies & Dunnavant.
    1853?
Rivelanti.
    1822.
Roberts.
    1896.
Rochambeau.
    1782.
Rollinson.
    1795.
    1795?
Roose.
    1876.
    1880.
    1881.
    1888.

MAPS AND VIEWS OF DISTRICT OF COLUMBIA

Ruebsam.
    1882.
Russell.
    1795.
Sachse.
    1852.
    1870.
    1871.
Sanborn map and publishing co.
    1888.
Schoeff.
    1891.
    1892.
Schwarz.
    1803?
Sears.
    1831.
Seibert.
    1791.
    1870.
Shanahan.
    1891.
Sheppard.
    1872.
Silversparre.
    1887.
Sinclair.
    1845.
Smith.
    1837.
    1862.
    1863.
Smithsonian park.
    1882.
Société de géographie. Paris.
    1829.
Standard atlas
    1888.
Stansbury.
    1827?
Stelwagen & Wolf.
    1892.
Stewart.
    1792.
    1894.

Stockdale.
    1794.
    1798.
Stone.
    1820.
    1852.
Streeter.
    1850.
Strickland.
    1814.
Swinton & Harrower.
    1884.
Sylvester
    1898.
Symons.
    1889.
Tannner.
    1836.
Tardieu.
    1808.
    1815.
Thackara & Vallance.
    1792.
    1794.
Thomas.
    1798.
Thornton.
    1793-1811.
    1803.
Tiebout.
    1792.
Todd & Brown.
    1868.
Toner.
    1791.
    1870.
Townsend.
    1885.
United States. Congress House of representatives.
    1826.
    1827.
    1876.
    1896.
    1897.

MAPS AND VIEWS OF DISTRICT OF COLUMBIA

United States. Congress House of representatives - continued.
   1898.
United States. Congress. Senate.
   1852.
United States. War department.
   1861.
   1862.
   1865.
Universal magazine.
   1793.
Vail.
   1826.
Vance.
   1824.
Van Derveer.
   1850.
   1851.
Varnum.
   1846.
   1854.
Viele.
   1890.
Waite publishing co.
   1896.
Walker.
   1870.
Ward.
   1882.
Warden.
   1815.
   1819.
Warner.
   1886.
Waters.
   1863.
Watters.
   1897.
Watterson.
   1814.

Weishampel.
   1876.
Weld.
   1798.
Wells.
   1863.
Werner co.
   1895.
Wilkinson.
   1814.
William.
   1897.
Williams.
   1826.
Willis.
   1839.
Wilson.
   1894.
Winchester.
   1792.
Winterbotham.
   1795.
Wittemann.
   1886.
Woodbridge.
   1831.
   1833.
Wyckoff.
   1894.
Wyeth.
   1876.
   1881.
Wyld.
   1814.
Young.
   1824.
   1835.
   1851.
   1862.
   1888.

MAPS AND VIEWS OF DISTRICT OF COLUMBIA

1782. [PW 1]
Amérique campagne 1782. Plans des differents camps occupés par l'armée aux ordres de mr. le comte de Rochambeau. Manuscript. [anon.] title. 54 colored plans. fol. 12 1/4 x 8 1/4 inches. [1782].

Note.–Plate 15, Camp à Alexandrie le 17 juillet. Plate 16, Camp à 1 mille audela de George's Town, Plate 17, Camp à Blandens'burg le 19 juillet.

1789. [PW 2]
A survey of the roads of the United States of America. By Christopher Colles. 1789 C. Tiebout, sculp. 1 p. 1. Sheet 1-86 (wants sheets 34-39) sq. 12mo. [New York, 1789].

Note.–Sheet 62-63, from Annapolis to Bladensburg; sheet 64-65, from Annapolis to Alexandria. Interesting as showing roads previous to the founding of Washington.

1791. [PW 3]
A map of the Genesee tract, in the county of Ontario, & state of New York; shewing its distance from & water communication with New York. Philadelphia & Baltimore; –also its distance from the new city of Columbia, [Washington], or the proposed seat of government of the United States. [anon.] 13 x 8 1/4. [n. p. 1791].

Note.–Gives "Columbia, the new seat of government of the United States."

1791. [PW 4]
Map of the middle states of North America, shewing the position of the Geneseo country comprehending the counties of Ontario & Steuben as laid off in townships of six miles square each. [anon.] Maverick sculpt.– 65 Liberty street, N. Y. 15 x 15 1/2. [New York 1791].

Note.–Gives Columbia or the Federal city and mentions "land sold in 1791 by the state of New York."

1791. [PW 5]
Map of the middle states of North America with part of Canada shewing the situation of the principal towns, viz: Columbia, Baltimore, Philadelphia, New York, Newport, (Rhode Island) Boston & Montreal also their several communications with respect to lake Ontario [anon.] 15 1/2 x 12 1/2.

Note. –Gives "Columbia or Washington the capital of America".

MAPS AND VIEWS OF DISTRICT OF COLUMBIA

1791. [PW 6]

Plan of Carrollsburg. Scale 100 ft. to one inch. 22 1/2 x 15.

[In Faehtz (E. F. M.) and Pratt (F. W.) Washington in embryo; or the National Capital from 1791 to 1800. sm. fol. [Washington, Gibson brothers, printers, 1874].

1791. [PW 7]

Plan of Hamburgh. Scale 200 ft. to one inch. 14 3/4 x 18 1/2.

[In Faehtz (E. F. M.) and Pratt (F. W.) Washington in embryo; or the National Capital from 1791 to 1800. sm. fol. [Washington, Gibson brothers, printers]. 1874.

1791. [PW 8]

Sketch of Washington in embryo, viz; previous to its survey by major L'Enfant. Compiled from the rare historical researches of dr. Joseph M. Toner. Compilers E. F. M. Faehtz & F. W. Pratt, 1874. 16 x 20.

[In Faehtz (E. F. M.) and Pratt (F. W.) Washington in embryo. fol. Washington, 1874. facing pp. 32].

1791. [PW 9]

Sketch of Washington in embryo viz, previous to its survey by major L'Enfant, 1792. Compiled from the rare historical researches of dr. Joseph M. Toner, who by special favor has permitted the use of his labor and materials for the publication of a grand historical map of the District now in progress by his efforts combined with the skill of S. R. Seibert, c. e., 1874. 8 x 10.

[In Washington, D. C. Capitol centennial committee. Centennial anniversary of the laying of the cornerstone of the National Capitol, sept. 18, 1793. 12mo. Washington, 1893. at end].

1791. [PW 10]

Plan of the city intended for the permanent seat of the government of t[he] United States. Projected agreeable to the direction of the president of the United States, in pursuance of an act of congress, passed the 16th day of july, 1790, "establishing the permanent seat on the bank of the Potowmac". By Peter Charles L'Enfant. [Reproduced from ms. of 1791]. 31 1/2 x 47. [Washington, 1887].

[United States. Treasury department. Coast and geodetic survey. Chart 3035[a]]

Note.–Another copy bound with "The King plats. Original in the "office of commissioner of public buildings". An incorrect reproduction was made under the seal of the commissioner of public buildings, certified oct. 10, 1882.

The Gazettee of the United States, for January 4, 1792, published in Philadelphia, has the following:

MAPS AND VIEWS OF DISTRICT OF COLUMBIA

New City Of Washington

The following description is annexed to the plan of the City of Washington, in the district of Columbia, as sent to Congress by the President some days ago.

Plan of the City intended for the permanent seat of the Government of the United States, projected agreeably to the direction of the President of the United States, in pursuance of an Act of Congress, passed on the 16th of July, 1790, "establishing the permanent seat on the banks of the Potowmack "- By Peter Charles L' Enfant.

OBSERVATIONS EXPLANATORY OF THE PLAN.

I. The positions for the different grand edifices, and for the several grand squares or areas of different shapes as they are laid down, were first determined on the most advantageous ground commanding the most extensive prospects, and the better susceptible of such improvements as the various interests of the several objects may require.

II. Lines or avenues of direct communication have been devised to connect the separate and most distant objects with the principals, and to preserve through the whole a reciprocity of sight at the same time. Attention has been paid to the passing of those leading avenues over the most favorable ground for prospect and convenience.

III. North and south lines, intersected by others running due east and west, make the distribution of the city into streets, squares, &c. and those lines have been so combined as to meet at certain given points with those divergent avenues, so as to form on the spaces "first determined", the different squares, or areas, which are all proportional in magnitude to the number of avenues leading to them.

BREADTH OF THE STREETS

Every grand transverse avenue, and every principal divergent one, such as the communication from the President's House to the Congress House, &c. are 160 feet in breadth, and thus divided:

	Feet.
10 feet for pavements on each side is	20
30 of gravel walk, planted with trees on each side	60
80 in the middle for carriage way	<u>80</u>
	160
The other streets are of the following dimensions, viz:	
Those leading to the public buildings or markets	130
Others	110 or 90

In order to execute the above plan, Mr. Ellicott drew a true meridian line by celestial observation, which passes through the area intended for the Congress-House; this line be crossed by another due east and west, and which passes through the same area. These lines were accurately measured, and made the basis on which the whole plan was executed. He ran all the lines by a transit instrument, and determined the acute angles by actual measurement and left nothing to uncertainty of the compass.

REFERENCES.

A. The equestrian figure of George Washington, a monument voted in 1783, by the late Continental Congress.

B. An historic column–also intended for a mile or itinerary column, from whose station (at a mile from the federal House) all distances and places through the continent are to be calculated.

C. A naval itinerary column, proposed to be erected to celebrate the first rise of a navy, and to stand a ready monument to perpetuate its progress and atchievments [sic].

D. A church intended for national purposes, such as public prayer, thanksgivings, funeral orations, &c. and assigned to the special use of no particular sect or denomination, but equally open to all. It will likewise be a proper shelter for such monuments as were voted by the late Continental Congress, for those heros who fell in the cause of liberty, and for such others as may hereafter be decreed by the voice of a grateful nation.

E.E. E. E. E. Five grand fountains, intended with a constant spout of water. N. B. There are within the limits of the city 25 good springs of excellent water, abundantly supplied in the driest season of the year.

F. A grand cascade, formed of the water of the sources of the Tiber.

G. G. Public walk, being a square of 1200 feet, through which carriages may ascend to the upper square of the Federal House.

H. A grand avenue 400 feet in breadth, and about a mile in length, bordered with gardens ending in a slope from the houses on each side: this avenue leads to the monument A. and connects the Congress garden with the

I. President's park and the

K. Well improved field, being a part of the walk from the President's house of about 1800 feet in breadth, and three fourths of a mile in length. Every lot deep colored red, with green plots, designates some of the situations which command the most agreeable prospects, and which are best calculated for spacious houses and gardens, such as may accommodate foreign ministers, &c.

L. Around this square and along the

M. Avenue from the two bridges to the federal house the pavements on each side will pass under an arched way, under whose cover shops will be most conveniently and agreeably situated: this street is 160 feet in breadth and a mile long.

The fifteen squares colored yellow, are proposed to be divided among several states in the Union, for each of them to improve, or subscribe a sum additional to the value of the land for that purpose, and improvements round the squares to be completed in a limited time.

The centre of each square will admit of statues, columns, obelisks, or any other ornaments, such as the different states may choose to erect, to perpetuate not only the memory of such individuals whose councils or military atchievments were conspicuous in giving liberty and independence to this country; but those whose usefulness hath rendered them worthy of imitation; to invite the youth of succeeding generations to tread in the paths of those sages or heroes whom their country have thought proper to celebrate.

The situation of those squares is such, that they are the most advantageously and reciprocally seen from each other, and as equally distributed over the whole city district, and connected by spacious avenues round the grand federal improvements, and as contiguous to them, and at the same time as equally distant from each other as circumstances would admit. The settlements round these squares must soon become connected.

The mode of taking possession of, and improving the whole district at first, must leave to posterity a grand idea of the patriotic interest which promoted it.

The small spaces colored red, are intended for the use of all religious denominations, on which they are to erect places of worship, and are proposed to be allotted to them in the manner as those coloured yellow are to the different states in the Union; but no burying ground will be admitted within the limits of the city, an appropriation being intended for that purpose without.

N. B. There are a number of squares or areas un appropriated, and in situations proper for Colleges and Academies, of which every society, whose object is national, may be accommodated. Every house within the city will stand square on the streets, and every lot on the divergent avenues will run square with their fronts on the most acute angle, will not measure less than 56 feet, and may well be above 140. Some of the streets running north and south, and east and west, are about 1200 poles, and the transverse streets about 1300 poles.

LATITUDE OF CONGRESS HOUSE, 38. 53 N. LONG. 0. 0.

X. Tiber creek. The water of this creek is intended to be conveyed on the high ground where the Congress-House stands, and after watering that part of the city, its overplus will fall from under the base of the edifice, and in a cascade of 20 feet in heighth, and 50 in breadth, into the reservoir below, thence to run in three falls through the gardens into the grand canal.

The perpendicular heighths of the ground where the Congress house stands, is above the tide of Tiber creek 78 feet.

Perpendicular heighth of the west branch above the tide of Tiber creek, 115 feet, 7 inches and two eights.

This branch and that of the Tiber, is intended to be conveyed to the President's house.

From the entrance of the river Potowmack up to the second, the depth of water is from 5 1/3 to 4 fathoms–the deepest all along the shore where wharves are marked.

1792. [PW 11]

Plan of the city of Washington, in the territory of Columbia, ceded by the states of Maryland and Virginia, [etc.] 1800. 17 x 19 1/2.

[In District of Columbia. Maps and plans. fol. Washington, A. B. Hamilton, 1852. at end].

Note.–The Andrew Ellicott plan.

1792. [PW 12]

Map of the city of Washington in the District of Columbia, showing the lines of the various properties at the division with the original proprietors in 1792. Colored. 23 x 30 1/2. Washington, J. M. Stewart, 1884.

1792. [PW 13]

Plan of the city of Washington. S. Hill, Boston. 8 x 11.

[In Massachusetts (The) magazine. May, 1792. 8vo. Boston, I. Thomas & E. T. Andrews, 1792. v. 4. p. 282].

Note.–The number for Dec., 1791, page 725, has a "Description of the city of Washington."

1792. [PW 14]

Plan of the city of Washington in the territory of Columbia ceded by the states of Virginia and Maryland to the United States of America, and by them established as the seat of their government after the year 1800. 21 x 29. Philadelphia, engrav'd by Thackara & Vallance, 1792.

Note.–This engraving by Thackara & Vallance, of Andrew Ellicott's plan, is the official plan of the city and has been repeatedly reproduced. A copy is bound with The King plats–1803 reproduced by the Coast and Geodetic survey.

MAPS AND VIEWS OF DISTRICT OF COLUMBIA

1792. [PW 15]

Plan of the city of Washington. 9 x 11.

[In Winchester (Elhahan). An oration on the discovery of America, delivered in London, October the 12th, 1792, being three hundred years from the day on which Columbus landed in the New World. The second edition with an appendix, containing among other things a description of the city of Washington, in the District of Columbia; illustrated with an accurate engraving. 12mo. London, for the author, [1792].

Note.–On pp. 49-52 is a descriptive text entitled "Description of the city of Washington, in the Territory of Columbia" [etc.] Page 48 contains an explanation of the plan.

1792. [PW 16]

Plan of the city of Washington. Tiebout [engraver]. 10 1/2 x 8.

[In New York (The) magazine; or, literary repository, june, 1792. 8vo. New York, T. & J. Swords. 1792. v. 3. p. 321].

Note.–On back of title page the following: "The reader is requested to turn to the New York magazine for november, 1791, for a description of the city of Washington. We have not seen any other account of this place, that would serve as an explanation of the plate which accompanies this month's magazine, but what is there contained in substance; and we judged it inexpedient to republish either the whole or any part of what has been so recently inserted". Originally published in the Maryland Journal, Sept. 30, 1791. Probably the first article published relating to Washington. Also published in Gazette of the United States, for October 8, 1791.

1792? [PW 17]

Plan of the city of Washington in the territory of Columbia, ceded by the states of Virginia and Maryland to the United States and by them established as the seat of their government after the year 1800. 17 x 22. Boston, engrav'd by Sam'l Hill, [1792]?

Note.–The Andrew Ellicott plan.

1792-1794. [PW 18]

Front elevation of the Federal Capitol. Plan B. submitted to the President by Stephen Hallet, 1792-1794. 14 1/4 x 39. manuscript.

Division of Prints.

1792-1794. [PW 19]

Front elevation of the Federal Capitol. Plan C. submitted by Stephen Hallet to President Jefferson–1792–1794. 14 1/4 x 45 1/2. Colored manuscript. Art Division.

1792-1794. [PW 20]

Principal floor of plan B. for Federal Capitol by Stephen Hallet. 18 x 40. Manuscript. Art Division.

MAPS AND VIEWS OF DISTRICT OF COLUMBIA

1792-1794. [PW 21]
Principal floor of plan C. for Federal Capitol by Stephen Hallet. 14 1/2 x 40 1/4. Art Division.

1792-1801. [PW 22]
Ground plan for the Capitol. Designed by Stephen L. Hallet. Accepted by the commissioners, 1792. "Leaving the east front recess open for further consideration". Rec'd from James Greenleaf as Hallet's original design of the Capitol. H. B. Latrobe, Phila. 1801. 16 1/2 x 22. Manuscript.
Division of Prints.

1793. [PW 23]
[Map of Duddington manor]. Laid down by a scale of eighty equal parts in an inch. By John F. A. Priggs, survr. 1793. ms. 14 x 17 1/2. 1793.

1793. [PW 24]
Plan of the city of Washington; now building for the metropolis of America, and established as the permanent residence of congress after the year 1800. B. Baker sculp. Published by W. Bent, 1793. 10 1/2 x 13 1/2.
[In Universal (The) magazine. 8vo. London, W. Bent, 1793, v. 93. july 1793, facing p. 41].

1793? [PW 25]
Territory of Columbia. Drawn by Andw. Ellicott. 1 sheet. fold. 22 x 22. [n. p. 1793]?
Note:–The first topographical survey of the District. The Library has three of the original copies and the reproduction no. 3059 made by U. S. Coast and Geodetic survey. Also found in "Maps of the District of Columbia, 1852," without name of author or date. During the year 1792, the commissioners employed Andrew Ellicott to survey the boundary lines of the Federal District, and on January 1, 1793, he made the following report of the survey to them:
"It is with singular satisfaction that I announce to you the completion of the survey of the four lines comprehending the Territory of Columbia. These lines are opened and cleared forty feet wide; that is, twenty feet on each side of the lines limiting the Territory; and in order to perpetuate the work, I have set up square milestones, marked progressively with the number of miles from the beginning on Jones's Point to the west corner; thence from the west corner; thence from the north corner to the east corner, and thence to the place of beginning on Jones's Point, except as to a few cases where the miles terminated on a declivity or in water; in such cases the stones are placed on the nearest firm ground, and their true distances in miles and poles marked on them. On the sides facing the Territory is inscribed, 'Jurisdiction of the United States'; on the opposite sides of those placed in the State of Virginia is inscribed 'Virginia', and of those in the State of Maryland is inscribed 'Maryland.' On the fourth side is inscribed the year and the present

MAPS AND VIEWS OF DISTRICT OF COLUMBIA

position of the magnetic needle at the place. With this you will receive a map of the four lines, with a half mile on each side, to which is added a survey of the waters in the Territory and a plan of the city of Washington."

This report evidently refers to the above map, of which there has been some question as to date of making.

1793? [PW 26]

Ellicott (Andrew). Territory of Columbia. [anon.] 22 x 22.

[In District of Columbia. Maps and plans. fol. Washington, A. B. Hamilton, 1852. at end].

Note:–A reproduction of the 1793? edition, without name of author or date. Also reproduced from the original copy in the Library of Congress, by the Coast and Geodetic survey. No. 3059.

1793-1811. [PW 27]

Ground plan of the Capitol. Designed by dr. Thornton, 1793. Accepted by the commissioners to modify the plan by Stephen L. Hallet, already approved with one exception. This plan was afterwards almost entirely adopted. Mr. Hallet being engaged as supervising architect at a salary of $400 a year. He resigned however, in a few months and mr. George Hadfield aided by mr. Jas. Hoban, architect of the White House built the north wing, completing it in 1800. The south wing was constructed under the supervision of architect Benj. H. Latrobe and finished in 1811. Plan of the Capitol rec'd from dr. Thornton, april, 1804. 17 x 24. Manuscript.

Division of Prints.

1794. [PW 28]

Front elevation of the Federal Capitol. Plan D. Submitted to President Jefferson by Stephen Hallet. 1794. 20 x 40.

Division of Prints.

1794. [PW 29]

Map of the state of Maryland laid down from an actual survey of all the principal waters, public roads, and divisions of the countries therein; describing the situation of the cities, towns, villages, houses of worship and other public buildings, furnaces, forges, mills and other remarkable places; and of the Federal territory; and also a sketch of the state of Delaware; showing the probable connexion of the Chesapeake and Delaware bays; by Dennis Griffith. June 20th. 1794. Engraved by J. Thackara & J. Vallance. Scale of miles 68 9/10 to a degree. 29 x 51. Philadelphia, J. Vallance, 1795.

Note: –Inset "Plan of the city of Washington and territory of Columbia". 22 x 22.

MAPS AND VIEWS OF DISTRICT OF COLUMBIA

[PW29a]
Plan of the city of Washington. 6 1/2 x 8 1/4. [London]. J. Stockdale. 16 sept. 1794.

[In Morse (Jedidiah). Maps of America, to accompany "The american geography. A new ed." [anon.] 12mo. London, for J. Stockdale, 1792-1794. no. 6].

1794. [PW 30]
Principal floor of plan D. for Federal Capitol by Stephen Hallet. 24 x 40. Manuscript.   Division of Prints.

1795. [PW 31]
Plan de la ville de Washington en Amérique. 6 1/2 x 7 3/4.

[In Gothaischer hof-kalender, 1795. 24mo. Gotha, [1795]. facing p. 94].

1795. [PW 32]
Plan of the city of Washington in the territory of Columbia ceded by the states of Virginia and Maryland and by them established as the seat of government after the year 1800. Rollinson sculpt. N. York. 16 x 20 1/2 Published by I. Reid, L. Warland and C. Smith, 1795.

[Inserted at end of The American atlas [to Winterbotham's history]. fol. New York, John Reid, 1796].

Note:–The Ellicott map with Potomac river soundings.

1795. [PW 33]
Plan of the city of Washington, in the territory of Columbia, ceded by the states of Virginia and Maryland to the United States of America and by them established as the seat of their government, after the year 1800. J. Russell sculpt. 15 1/2 by 20 1/2.

[In Russell (J.) An American atlas. fol. London, H. D. Symonds & J. Ridgway, 1795. at end].

Note.–The Ellicott map with Potomac river soundings. Published without date.

1795. [PW 34]
Plan of the city of Washington in the territory of Columbia ceded by the states of Virginia and Maryland to the United States and by them established as the seat of their government, after the year 1800. Published by I. Reid. 16 by 20 1/2. New York, Rollinson, sculpt. [1795]?

Note.–The Ellicott map with Potomac river soundings. Published without date.

Maps and Views of District of Columbia

1796. [PW 35]

The red shade shews the part of Port Royal belonging to mess'rs Sands & Lynch. City of Washington, June 9th, 1796. James R. Dermott. Scale 200 feet in inch. 24 by 20 1/4.

Note.–Manuscript map showing blocks 366-563, situated between north K. and North 0. streets, including parts of New York, New Jersey and Massachusetts avenues.

1797-98. [PW 36]

Dermott (James R.) The Dermott or tin-case map of the city of Washington 1797-8. 53 x 61 3/4.

Note.–Plan of the city to which was attached, two papers one signed by George Washington, march 2, 1797, the other by John Adams, july 23, 1798. Original in the office of commissioner of public buildings. Reproduced by the Coast and Geodetic survey in separate sheets and also in bound volume of "King plats 1803."

1798. [PW 37]

Plan of the city of Washington. 7 x 8 1/2. London, J. Stockdale, 1798.

[In Weld (Isaac). Travels through the states of North America. 8vo. London, 1810. v. 1. p. 81].

1798. [PW 38]

Plan of the town of Alexandria in the District of Columbia. 1798. 19 x 23 1/2. Alexandria, published by I. V. Thomas, New York, engraved by T. Clarke, [1798].

Note.–Drawn by Colonel George Gilpin.

1802. [PW 39]

The traveller's directory; or, a pocket companion. By S. S. Moore & T. W. Jones. 2 p. 1. 52 pp. 25 maps. Philadelphia, M. Carey, 1802.

Note.–Showing roads from Phila. to N. Y. and from Phila. to Wash. Also plan of Washington. Second edition published in 1804.

1803. [PW 40]

During the short residence of President Adams at Washington the wooden stairs & platform were the usual entrance to the house, and the present drawing-room was a mere vestibule. Plan of the principal story in 1803. B. Henry Latrobe, S. P. B. U. S. 1807. 18 x 14.

Division of Prints.

MAPS AND VIEWS OF DISTRICT OF COLUMBIA

1803. [PW 41]

Ground plan for the Capitol. Designed by dr. Thornton showing the use for which each chamber was intended. Given to architect Benj. H. Latrobe by mr. Geo. Blagden as the only existing drawing of the Capitol, may 4, 1803. B. H. Latrobe. 16 x 20 1/4. Manuscript.

Division of Prints.

1803. [PW 42]

The Kings plats of the city of Washington in the District of Columbia, 1803. With L' Enfant, Ellicott's and Dermott's maps appended. 2 p. 1. 21 sheets. fol. Washington, N. Peters, photo. lith. [1888].

Note.–Original in the War Department. Reproduced by the Coast and Geodetic survey.

1803. [PW 43]

Plan of principal story in 1803. [White House]. B. Henry Latrobe S. P. B. U. S.

Manuscript diagram in the Art Division, with following text at top. "The surrounding yard was chiefly used for brick yards, it was enclosed in a rough post and rail fence. (1803)." At bottom. "During the residence of president Adams at Washington, the wooden stairs & platform were the usual entrance to the house, and the present drawing room, was a mere vestibule". 17 1/2 x 13 1/2.

1803? [PW 44]

A map of the city of Washington in the District of Columbia, established as the permanent seat of government of the United States of America. Taken from actual survey, as laid out on the ground. By Rt. King. 24 x 31. Washington, engraved by C. Schwarz. [1803]?

Note.–Inset view of "South front of the President's house as designed and executed by James Hoban" and East front of the Capitol as originally designed by William Thornton." No date given to this map. Presumably 1803.

1803? [PW 45]

King (Robert). Part of the city of Washington shewing the height of the present surface of the ground from Pennsylvania ave to New Jersey avenue below the Capitol hill. Manuscript. 19 x 23.

1804. [PW 46]

The traveller's directory; or, a pocket companion, shewing the course of the main road from Philadelphia to New York; and from Philadelphia to Washington: with descriptions of the places through which it passes. From actual survey. By S. S. Moore and T. W. Jones. 2d ed. title. 37, 19

MAPS AND VIEWS OF DISTRICT OF COLUMBIA

pp. 23 pl. 8vo. Philadelphia for Matthew Carey, 1804.
    Note.–Plan of Washington on sheet 23. First edition published in 1802.

1805. [PW 47]
Ground plan for the Capitol. Designed by dr. Thornton showing how the project for putting offices under the Hall of representatives might be effected. Mr. Jefferson on putting this plan into my hands stated that he had communicated with dr. Thornton on the plan submitted by me for putting a story of offices under the Hall of representatives, & that dr. Thornton had in consequence given him this plan as showing how the project might be effected. But at that time my plan was already in progress. B. H. Latrobe, Feb. 1st. 1805. Rec'd by B. H. Latrobe from President U. States. Jan'r 12th 1805. 18 x 21. Manuscript.
                                              Division of Prints.

1807. [PW 48]
Front view of the President's house, in the city of Washington.
    [On title page of Janson (Charles William). The stranger in America. 4to. London, Cundee, 1807].

1807. [PW 49]
Plan of the principal story, as proposed to be altered. B. Henry Latrobe, suvr. pub. bldg. U. S. 1807 A manuscript plan of the White House interior and exterior, showing diagram of rooms, south & north entrance etc. 17 1/2 x 13 1/2.

1807. [PW 50]
View of the east front of the president's house with the addition of the north & south porticos. H. B. Latrobe. 1807. S. P. B. U. States. 13 1/2 x 17 3/4. Colored ms. view in the Division of Prints, Library of Congress.

1807-1817. [PW 51]
Elevation of the south front of the President's house copied from the design as proposed to be altered in 1807. Jan. 1817. B. H. Latrobe. 13 1/2 x 18. Colored manuscript.   Division of Prints.

1808. [PW 52]
Plan de la ville de Washington située sur le territoire de Columbia cedé par les états de Virginie et Maryland aux États Unis. 9 1/4 x 12 1/2.
    [Inset Arrowsmith (Aaron). Carte des États Unis, copiée et gravée sur celle d'Arrowsmith. Par P. F. Tardieu. Paris, 1808].

Maps and Views of District of Columbia

1810. [PW 53]

South elevation of the Capitol U. S. Washington. Scale 16 feet to an inch. B. H. Latrobe, 1810. 19 x 29. Colored manuscript.

Division of Prints.

1811. [PW 54]

Graduation of 17th street west, showing the continuation of the war office drain. N. King. 11th may, 1805. ms. 15 x 20. [n. p. 1811].

1811. [PW 55]

The part of a circle at the meeting of Pennsylvania & Kentucky avenues on the Eastern branch. Calculated march, 1811. [anon.] ms. 13 x 18. [n. p. 1811].

1811. [PW 56]

Proposed designs for U. S. Capitol by architect Benjamen H. Latrobe, 1811. West elevation of the Capitol U. S. Washington. B. H. Latrobe, Feb. 4, 1811. 18 1/2 x 29 1/2. Colored manuscript. Division of Prints.

1814. [PW 57]

The affair of Bladensburg, aug. 21, 1814. 6 x 7.

[In Wilkinson (James). Diagrams and plans illustrative of the principal battles and military affairs treated of in Memoirs of my own times. 4to. Philadelphia, 1816. no. 17].

1814. [PW 58]

Capitol, after its destruction by the British-aug. 24th, 1814. 3 1/2 x 6.

[In Washington, D. C. Capitol centennial committee. Centennial anniversary of the laying of the corner-stone of the National Capitol, sept. 18, 1793. 12mo. Washington, 1893. p. 6].

1814. [PW 59]

The Capitol in 1814, from Pennsylvania avenue. 3 x 5 3/4.

[In Washington, D. C. Capitol centennial committee. Centennial anniversary of the laying of the corner-stone of the National Capitol, sept. 18, 1793. 12mo. Washington, 1893. p. 5].

1814. [PW 60]

President's house, after its destruction by the British. 3 1/4 x 5.

[In Watterson (George). New guide to Washington, R. Farnham, 1847-8. p. 57].

MAPS AND VIEWS OF DISTRICT OF COLUMBIA

1814. [PW 61]

Sketch of the march of the British army under gen'l Ross. From the 19th to the 29th august, 1814. From a sketch by D. Evans, lt. 3d. dr'ns as't or. mas'r gen'l. Military depot quarter mas'r gen'l office horse guards, oct'r 10th, 1814. J. Wyld, [engraver, London]. 18 1/2 x 13 3/4.

Note.–Inset "Sketch of the engagement on the 24th of august 1814 between the British and American forces." Original engraving.

1814. [PW 62]

Sketch of the march of the british army under gen'l Ross. From the 19th to the 29th august, 1814. From a sketch by D. Evans, lt. 3d dr'ns dy. ast. fr. mas't gen'l. Military depot quarter masr. gen'l office Horse guards, oct. 10th, 1847. J. Wyld. T. Sinclair's lith. Phila. 18 1/4 x 13 3/4.

[In Ingram (E. D.) A sketch of the events which preceded the capture of Washington. [By E. D. I. anon.] 8vo. Philadelphia, Carey & Hart, 1849. front.]

Note.–Inset "Sketch of the engagement on the 24th of august, 1814 between the British and American forces."

1814. [PW 63]

Map of maj. gen. Ross' route with the british column, from Benedict, on the Patuxent river, to the city of Washington, aug. 1814. 13 1/2 x 15. [London] W. James, may 11, 1818.

[In James (William). A full and correct account of the military occurrences of the late war between Great Britain and the United States. 8vo. London, for the author, 1818. v. 2. face title page].

1814. [PW 64]

Map of maj: gen: Ross's route with the british column, from Benedict, on the Patuxent river, to the city of Washington, aug. 1814. 14 x 16.

[In Wilkinson (James). Diagrams and plans illustrative of the principal battles and military affairs treated of in Memoirs of my own times. 4to. Philadelphia, 1816 no. 16].

1814. [PW 65]

A view of the Capitol of the United States after the conflagration of the 24th august 1814. G. Munger, del. –W. Strickland, sculp. 11 1/2 x 17. Colored.   Division of Prints.

1814. [PW 66]

A view of the President's house in the city of Washington after the conflagration of the 24th august, 1814. G. Munger, del. W. Strickland, sculp. 10 1/2 x 17. Colored manuscript.   Division of Prints.

Maps and Views of District of Columbia

1815. [PW 67]

Map, exhibiting the property of the U. S. in the vicinity of the Capitol, colored red, with the manner in which it is proposed to lay off the same in building lots, as described in the report of the supt. of the city to which this is annexed. B. W. Latrobe, one of the surveyors of the city of Washington. Dec. 3, 1815. ms. 18 1/2 x 23.

1815. [PW 68]

Territory of Columbia. Drawn by Andw. Ellicott. Engraved by P. A. F. Tardieu. Paris, 1815. 10 1/2 x 10 1/2.

[In Warden (D. B.) A chorographical and statistical description of the District of Columbia. 8vo. Paris, Smith, 1816].

Note.–The Ellicott topographical map 1793? The author on p. 34, mentions the "plan of major L' Enfant, engraved at the expense of the government on a scale of a hundred poles to an inch." Between pp. 34 -35 is a view of the Capitol 3 1/4 x 8 1/4 inches. Detournelle del. et sculp.

1815. [PW 69]

View of the Capitol. Detournelle, del. et sculp.

[In Warden (D. B.) A chorographical and statistical description of the District of Columbia. 8vo. Paris, Smith, 1816. bet. pp. 34-35].

1816. [PW 70]

The Capitol—Washington, 1816. Detournelle del. et sculp. 2 3/4 x 6.

[In Washington, D. C. Capitol centennial committee. Centennial anniversary of the laying of the corner-stone of the National Capitol, sept. 18, 1793. 12mo. Washington, 1893. p. 8].

1817. [PW 71]

The plan of the principal floor of the Capitol U. S. 1817. Those parts which are colored light red denote the walls remaining, and carried up since the conflagration of 1814. Those of a deeper red, the work commenced for the completion of the wings, agreeably to the suggestions of both houses of Congress. Those colored grey, are not ultimately determined and are submitted to the President, U. S. March 18, 1817. 21 x 30 1/2 Division of Prints.

1817. [PW 72]

Plan of the principal story of the north wing of the Capitol U. S. as authorised to be built, 1817. F. C. De Krafft, delin. 19 1/2 x 31. Colored manuscript. Division of Prints.

MAPS AND VIEWS OF DISTRICT OF COLUMBIA

1817. [PW 73]

Plan of the principal floor of the south wing of the Capitol as authorized to be built, 1817. B. H. Latrobe, scul. Wm. Blanchard, del. Colored. 21 x 9 1/2. Division of Prints.

1817. [PW 74]

Plan of wharfing, by B. H. Latrobe, surveyor city of Washington, March 3, 1817. ms. 17 x 22. [1817].

1818. [PW 75]

Plan of the city of Washington. 5 x 7 1/2.

[In Mackenzie (E.) An historical, etc. view of the United States. 8vo. Newcastle, 1818. facing p. 319].

1819. [PW 76]

Plan of the city of Washington. 5 x 7.

[In Mackenzie (E.) An historical, topographical, and descriptive view of the United States. 2d ed. 8vo. Newcastle upon Tyne, Mackenzie & Dent, 1819. facing p. 319].

1819. [PW 77]

Ground floor. principal floor, attic floor of the treasury and war office. Drawn by Wm. Blanchard, 1819. Manuscript. 19 1/2 x 16 1/2.

1819. [PW 78]

Plan of the city of Washington and territory of Columbia. Engraved by W. & D. Lizars, Edinr. 13 1/4 x 13 1/4.

[In Warden (D. B.) A statistical, political and historical account of the United States. 8vo. Edinburgh, 1819. v. 3. front.]

1820. [PW 79]

Bird's eye view of the new congress hall, showing the plan of the room and the position of the floor of the different members of the house of representatives. 4 3/4 x 7.

[In Atlantic (The) magazine. New series. March, 1820. 8vo. Philadelphia, J. Maxwell, 1820. v. 1. no. 3. p. 240].

Maps and Views of District of Columbia

1820. [PW 80]

A correct map of the city of Washington. Engd. by W. I. Stone, Wash. 16 x 21.

[In National (A) calendar for 1820. By Peter Force. 18mo. Washington, Davis & Force, 1820].

Note.–Inset views of "West front of the Capitol" and "North front of the President's house".

1820. [PW 81]

A front view of the president's house, Washington. Geo. Catlin, del. I. L. Frederick sc. 3 1/2 x 5 1/2.

[In Atlantic (The) magazine. New series. April, 1820. 8vo. Philadelphia, J. Maxwell, 1820. v. 1. no. 4. front].

1821. [PW 82]

West front of the Capitol. Engraved for the National calender, 1821. Drawn by C. Bullfinch, surveyor of the Capitol. 3 1/2 x 6.

[In Washington, D. C. Capitol centennial committee. Centennial anniversary of the laying of the corner-stone of the National Capitol, sept. 18, 1793. 12mo. Washington, 1893. p. 10].

1822. [PW 83]

Facciata del Campicoglio di Washington. S. Marceau, dis. A. Rivelanti, inc. 2 1/2 x 3 1/2

[In Compagnoni (G.) Storia del l'America. [anon.] 16mo. Milano, Fusi, Stella & co., 1822. v. 14 p. 58].

1822. [PW 84]

Geographical, statistical, and historical map of the District of Columbia. 11 x 10 1/2.

[In Complete (A.) historical, chronological and geographical american atlas. fol. Philadelphia, H. C. Carey & I. Lea, 1822. no. 21].

1822. [PW 85]

North front of the president's house. 3 x 5 3/4.

[In National (The) calendar. 1822. By Peter Force. 18mo. Washington, Davis & Force, 1822. front.]

Note:–Also views of the President's House, state, treasury, war and navy departments on page 227.

MAPS AND VIEWS OF DISTRICT OF COLUMBIA

1822. [PW 86]

Perimetro della cittá di Washington. S. Marceau, dis. A. Rivelanti, inc. 3 x 3 1/2.

[In Compagnoni (G.) Storia del l'America. [anon.] 16mo. Milano, Fusi, Stella e co., 1822. v. 14. p. 58].

1822. [PW 87]

Plan of the city of Washington, seat of government of the United States. Entered according to act of Congress on the 12 day of nov. 1822, by S. A. Elliot of the District of Columbia. 16 3/4 x 21.

[In Elliot (William). The Washington guide. [anon.] 18mo. Washington, S. A. Elliot, 1822].

Note.–The author states in preface "It was, no doubt, through the influence of general Washington, that the seat of the national government was established here; but it required the fostering hand of every successive administration to keep alive and nourish what he had so wisely planted. Happily this has been done to the extent of every reasonable man's expectation. The city was laid out during the administration of John Adams; of which the map in the front is a correct copy, and was signed by himself."

1822. [PW 88]

Plan shewing the present & proposed direction of the canal between 3d & seventh streets. Scale 200 ft. to an inch. F. C. de K[rafft.anon.] Aug. 7, 1822. ms. 18 x 23.

1822. [PW 89]

Plan shewing the present and proposed directions of the canal between 3d & 7th street west on the Mall. The above is a true copy from the original by F. C. de Krafft. Aug. 27, 1822. Scale 200 feet to an inch. ms. 15 x 17.

1823. [PW 90]

Plan of the principal floor of the Capitol. 6 x 8.

[In National (The) calendar for 1823. By Peter Force. 16mo. Washington, Davis & Force, 1823. front.]

1824. [PW 91]

Dimensions of that part of the Center Market square requiring to be filled in the 22nd june 1824. Manuscript. 11 1/2 x 15 3/4.

1824. [PW 92]

Map of Virginia and Maryland, constructed from the latest authorities.

MAPS AND VIEWS OF DISTRICT OF COLUMBIA

1824. Drawn by D. H. Vance. Engrav'd by J. H. Young. 17 x 22.
[In Finley (Anthony). A new american atlas. fol. Philadelphia, A. Finley, 1826, no. 7].
Note.–Insert "Plan of Washington & Georgetown."

1825. [[PW 93]

Oestliche fronte des capitols von Washington [&] Grundriss des capitols. C. Ermer sculp. 9 x 7 1/2.
[In Bernhard (Carl, herzog von Sachsen Weimar Eisenach). Reise durch Nord Amerika in 1825 und 1826. 8vo Weimar, W. Hoffmann, 1828. v. 1. p. 270].

1824. [PW 94]

Plan of the city of Washington. Laid down agreeably to the surveyor's returns. F. C. de Krafft, S. C. W. 1824. 16 sheets. folio.
Note.–Manuscript. Title on back of cover, "Plats of Washington 1-16." Force collection.

1824? [PW 95]

[Plats of Washington. anon.] 30 sheets. folio.
Note.–Manuscript without date, title, or surveyor's name. Title from cover. Presumably by F. C. de Krafft, surveyor, 1824.

1826. [PW 96]

Map of reconnaissance exhibiting the country between Washington and New Orleans with the routes examined in reference to a contemplated national road between these two cities. 20 x 26.
Note.–Map to accompany Doc. no. 156 [45] 19th. cong. 1st sess. Ho. of reps. Dept. War Road from Washington to New Orleans. 28 pages. Washington, 1826. Page 11 states "A general map has been compiled from Tanner's atlas, and drawn by lieuts. Jefferson Vail and W. Williams, of the infantry. The projection is that employed by Delille and Danville, and adopted by mr. Tanner, for his atlas: the scale is 10 miles to an inch."

1826. [PW 97]

Map of the country between Washington & Pittsburg referring to the contemplated Chesapeake & Ohio canal and its general route and profile, Oct. 1826. Reduced from the general map, annexed to the report upon the contemplated canal & drawn by lieut. Farley. Etched by Wm. Harrison. Georgetown, D. C. 17 x 25 1/2. [Georgetown, 1826].
Note.–From map 16, by E. H. Courtney, accompanying Doc. 83, 18th congress, 2d sess. 1825.

Maps and Views of District of Columbia

1826. [PW 98]
Plan of the grounds adjacent to the Capitol, shewing the projected alteration of the canal & the amount of land proposed to be laid into building lots. Scale 200 ft. to an inch. F. C. de Krafft. [anon.] ms. 18 1/2 x 28.
  Note.–Has newspaper cutting pasted on side explaining conditions of the scale.

1826. [PW 99]
Plan of the present city hall on the square between north D & E streets & between 4th and 5th streets west. F. C. de Krafft, surveyor c. Washington. Aug. 8, 1826. ms. 14 x 20.

1826. [PW 100]
Plan of squares marked A. & B. in mr. Bulfinch's plan. Scale 100 ft. to an inch. F. C. de K[rafft anon.] ms. 15 x 18.

1827. [PW 101]
Map of the country embracing the several routes examined with a view to a national road from Washington to Buffalo. 16 x 35.
  [In United States. Congress. Ho. of rep. Road from Washington to Buffalo. 8vo. Washington, 1827].
  Note.–Through Maryland, Penna. & New York.

1827. [PW 102]
Plan of the city of Washington, seat of government of the United States. 17 x 21.
  [In Washington, D. C. Directories. 1827. 16mo. Washington, S. A. Elliott, 1827].
  Note.–The plan copyrighted nov. 12, 1822 by S. A. Elliott.

1827? [PW 103]
Map of the country embracing the several routes examined with a view to a national road from Washington to lake Ontario. Compiled by A. J. Stansbury. 35 x 17. Georgetown, D. C., engraved by W. Harrison, [1827]?

1828. [PW 104]
East elevation of the Capitol. Completed 1828 under the supervision of Mr. Chas. Bulfinch and according to the design of architect Benj. H. Latrobe. Colored. 13 1/2 x 19 1/2. Art Division.

Maps and Views of District of Columbia

1828. [PW 105]
Map of the city of Washington. Published by John Brannan. 1828. Drawn by F. C. de Krafft, city surveyor. Engd. by mrs. W. I. Stone. 16 x 20 3/4. [Washington, published by J. Brannan, 1828].

1829. [PW 106]
Carte du pays compris entre Washington et Pittsburg, offrant le tracé général du canal de jonction de la baie de Chesapeak à la rivière d'Ohio, et ses profils. 10 3/4 x 16.
[In Société de géographie. Bulletin. 8vo. Paris, 1829. v. 11].

1830. [PW 107]
Capitol, Washington, 1830. From a sketch by Davis, N. Y. 3 1/2 x 6.
[In Washington, D. C. Capitol centennial committee. Centennial anniversary of the laying of the corner-stone of the National Capitol, sept. 18, 1793. 12mo. Washington, 1893. p. 12].

1830. [PW 108]
Capitol. West front, 1830. 3 1/2 x 6.
[In Washington, D. C. Capitol centennial committee. Centennial anniversary of the laying of the corner-stone of the National Capitol, sept. 18, 1793. 12mo. Washington, 1893. p. 14].

1830. [PW 109]
A map of Georgetown in the District of Columbia by William Bussard, 1830. Scale 100 yards to an inch. 23 1/2 x 29. Washington, engd. by W. Harrison, [1830].

1831. [PW 110]
Capitol of the U. S. Washington. West front. 4 1/2 x 5 3/4. Engraved & printed by Fenner, Sears & co. Drawn by W. Goodacre, N. Y. London, I. T. Hinton & Simpkin & Marshall, 1831.
[In Hinton (J. H.) The history and topography of the United States. 3d ed. 4to. London, J. Dowding, 1842. v.1. facing p. 458].

1831. [PW 111]
Capitol of the United States, Washington. Engraved & printed by Fenner Sears & co. Drawn by H. Brown. London, I. T. Hinton & Simpkin & Marshall, 1831. 3 3/4 x 6.
[In Hinton (J. H.) The history and topography of the United States. 3d ed. 4to. London, J. Dowding, 1842. v. 2. facing p. 527].

MAPS AND VIEWS OF DISTRICT OF COLUMBIA

1831. [PW 112]
The department of state, Washington. 4 x 5 3/4. Engraved & printed by Fenner, Sears & co. Drawn by C. Burton, N. Y. London, I. T. Hinton & Simpkin & Marshall.

[In Hinton (J. H.) The history and topography of the United States. 3d ed. 4to. London, J. Dowding, 1842. v. 1. facing p. 458].

1831. [PW 113]
Map of the states of Virginia and Maryland. 9 3/4 x 15 1/4. Engraved & printed by Fenner, Sears & co. London, I. T. Hinton & Simpkin & Marshall, 1831.

[In Hinton (J. H.) The history and topography of the United States. 3d ed. 4to. London, J. Dowding, 1842. v. 1. facing p. 17].

Note.–Inset "Plan of Washington and Georgetown".

1831. [PW 114]
Modern atlas on a new plan to accompany the system of universal geography; a new ed. improved by William Channing Woodbridge. 4th ed. 3 p. 1. 8 col. maps. front. 4to. Hartford, O. D. Cooke & co. 1831.

Note.–Inset views of the Capitol and White House on frontispiece.

1831. [PW 115]
The president's house, Washington. Engraved & printed by Fenner, Sears & co. Drawn by H. Brown. 4 x 6. London, I. T. Hinton & Simpkin & Marshall, 1831.

[In Hinton (J. H.) The history and topography of the United States. 3d ed. 4to. London, J. Dowding, 1842. v. 1. facing p. 458].

1831. [PW 116]
Woodbridge's school atlas; an improved ed. By William Channing Woodbridge. title. 9 maps. 4to. Hartford, O. D. Cooke & co. 1831.

Note.–At end "Washington city and its environs" Also found in the edition of 1833 and 1835.

1833. [PW 117]
Washington city and its environs. 4 x 3 1/2.

[In Woodbridge (William Channing). Woodbridge's school atlas. Improved ed. 4to. Hartford, O. D. Cook & co. 1833].

Maps and Views of District of Columbia

1834. [PW 118]
Capitol of the United States, Washington. H. Brown, del. 5 1/2 x 8 1/2.

[In Malte-Brun (Conrad). A system of universal geography. 4to. Boston, S. Walker, 1834. v. 2. front].

1834. [PW 119]
Capitol of the United States, Washington. J. Andrews, sc. Carter Andrews & co. H. Brown, del. Boston. 5 1/2 x 8.

[In Hinton (J. H.) The history and topography of the United States. New ed. 4to. Boston, Samuel Walker, 1834. v. 1. facing p. 220].

1834. [PW 120]
City of Washington. From beyond the Navy Yard. Published by Lewis P. Clover. Printed by G. Cook. Engd. by W. J. Bennett. Entered according to act of Congress in the year 1834 by Lewis P. Clover in the clerk's office of the district court of the southern district of New York. [View] colored. 18 1/2 x 24 1/2.   Art Division.

1834. [PW 121]
The president's house, Washington. J. Andrews, sc. Carter Andrews & Co. H. Brown, del. Boston. 5 1/4 x 8.

[In Hinton (J. H.) The history and topography of the United States. New ed. 4to. Boston, Samuel Walker, 1834. v.1. facing p. 240].

1834. [PW 122]
The president's house, Washington. H. Brown, del. J. Andrews, sc. 5 1/2 x 8 1/2.

[In Malte-Brun (Conrad). A system of universal geography. 8vo. Boston, S. Walker, 1834. v.2. p. 218].

1834. [PW 123]
Washington [View]. Drawn by J. R. Smith. Engraved by J. D. Neagle.

[In Malte-Brun (Conrad). A system of universal geography. 8vo. Boston, S. Walker, 1834. v. 2. p. 218].

1834-1835. [PW 124]
Front view of the Capitol. Washingon. 5 3/4 x 9.

[In American (The) magazine of useful and entertaining knowledge. [1834-1835]. 8vo. Boston, Berwick co. 1835. v. 1. p. 519].

Maps and Views of District of Columbia

1835. [PW 125]
District of Columbia. 10 x 7 1/2.

[In Bradford (Thomas G.) A comprehensive atlas, geographical, historical & commercial. 4to. Boston, W. D. Tichnor, [1835]. no. 37].

1835. [PW 126]
Engraved for the gazetteer of the state of Virginia, exhibiting its internal improvements, roads, distances &c. by J. H. Young. 12 1/2 x 15. Philadelphia, S. A. Mitchell, 1835.

[In Martin (Joseph). A new and comprehensive gazetteer of Virginia and the District of Columbia. 8vo. Charlottesville, J. Martin, 1835].

Note.–Inset "District of Columbia" Pages 471-512, contains descriptive text relating to Washington, Georgetown and Alexandria.

1836. [PW 127]
City of Washington. 11 1/2 x 14 1/2.

[In Tanner (H. S.) A new universal atlas. 4to. Philadelphia, author, 1836. no. 66].

Note.–Inset "Plan of the principal floor of the Capitol."

1837. [PW 128]
Department of state at Washington, D. C. 3 1/2 x 5 1/2.

[In American (The) magazine of useful and entertaining knowledge. [2d ed. 1837]. 8vo. Boston, J. L. Sibley, 1837. v. 1. p. 317].

1837. [PW 129]
Routes between New York & Washington. Drawn by I. Smith. 4 1/2 x 23. New York, J. Disturnell, 1837.

[In Disturnell (John). A guide between New York, Philadelphia, [etc]. 18mo. New York, J. Disturnell, 1837].

1837. [PW 130]
View of the Capitol at Washington. 5 1/2 x 8 1/2.

[In American (The) magazine of useful and entertaining knowledge, [1837]. 8vo. Boston, J. L. Sibley, 1837. v. 3. p. 26].

1837. [PW 131]
View of the president's house, at Washington. 4 x 6.

[In American (The) magazine of useful and entertaining knowledge, [1837]. 8vo. Boston, J. L. Sibley, 1837. v. 3. p. 78].

Maps and Views of District of Columbia

1838. [PW 132]

View of the city of Washington. The metropolis of the United States of America. Taken from Arlington house, the residence of George Washington P. Custis, esq. P. Anderson, del. On stone by F. H. Lane. 15 x 36 1/4. Boston, T. Moore, [1838].

1838. [PW 133]

Washington. 6 x 7.

[In Bradford (Thomas G.). An illustrated atlas, geographical, statistical and historical of the United States. fol. Boston, Weeks, Jordan & co. 1838. p. 33].

Note:—On the illustrated title page is a view of the Capitol and pp. 33-34, a descriptive text.

1839. [PW 134]

The Capitol. East view, 1839. 3 1/2 x 6.

[In Washington, D. C. Capitol centennial committee. Centennial anniversary of the laying of the corner-stone of the National Capitol, sept. 18, 1793. 12mo. Washington, 1893. p.16].

1839. [PW 135]

The president's house, from Washington. 4 3/4 x 7 1/4.

[In American scenery. From drawings by W. H. Bartlett. The literary department by N. P. Willis. 4to. London, G. Virtue, 1840. v. 2. p. 32].

1839. [PW 136]

Principal front of the Capitol, Washington. 5 x 7. London, G. Virtue, 1839.

[In American scenery. From drawings by W. H. Bartlett. The literary department by N. P. Willis. 4to. London, G. Virtue, 1840. v. 2. p. 55].

1839. [PW 137]

View of the Capitol at Washington. 5 x 7. London, G. Virtue, 1839.

[In American scenery. From drawings by W. H. Bartlett. The literary department by N. P. Willis. 4to. London, G. Virtue, 1840. v. 1. p. 36].

1839. [PW 138]

Washington, from the president's house. —Vue de Washington, pris de la maison du president. —Washington vom hotel des präsidenten gesehn. W. H. Bartlett. H. Wallis. 11 1/2 x 8 3/4. London, Geo: Virtue, 1839.

[In American scenery. From drawings by W. H. Bartlett. The literary department by N. P. Willis. 4to. London, G. Virtue, 1840. v. 2. p. 49].

MAPS AND VIEWS OF DISTRICT OF COLUMBIA

1840. [PW 139]
Ascent to the Capitol, Washington.
[In American scenery. From drawings by W. H. Bartlett. The literary department by N. P. Willis. 4to. London, G. Virtue, 1840. v. 1. title page].

1840. [PW 140]
The Capitol. From the Vigrinia (sic) side of the Potomac, 1840. 3 1/2 x 6.
[In Washington, D. C. Capitol centennial committee. Centennial anniversary of the laying of the corner-stone of the National Capitol, sept. 18, 1793. 12mo. Washington, 1893. p. 18].

1840. [PW 141]
View of the city of Washington.
[In Haas (P.) Public buildings and statuary of the government. 18mo. Washington, P. Haas, 1840].

1840? [PW 142]
The Capitol of the United States in Washington. H. Brown, del. 3 1/2 x 6 1/4.
[In Our globe. A universal picturesque album. obl. 4to. Philadelphia, edited by the North American bibliographic institution, 1840? p. 81].

1841. [PW 143]
Capitol. South west view, 1841. 3 1/2 x 6.
[In Washington, D. C. Capitol centennial committee. Centennial anniversary of the laying of the corner-stone of the National Capitol, sept. 18, 1793. 12mo. Washington, 1893. p. 22].

1841 [PW 144]
View of the White House.
[In Buckingham (J. S.) America. 8vo. London, Fisher & co. 1841. v. 1. p. 310].

1842. [PW 145]
Interior of the house of representatives, Washington. Drawn by W. Goodacre, N. Y. Engraved & printed by Fenner, Sears & co. 5 1/2 x 4 1/2.
[In Hinton (J. H.) The history and topography of the United States. 3d ed. 4to. London, J. Dowding, 1842. v. 2. facing p. 527].

MAPS AND VIEWS OF DISTRICT OF COLUMBIA

1845. [PW 146]
Plan of the town of Alexandria, D. C. with the environs. Exhibiting the outlet of the Alexandria canal the shipping channel, wharves, Hunting cr. &c. From actual survey by Maskell C. Ewing, 1845. 19 x 24. Philadelphia, lith. of T. Sinclair, [1845].
 Note.–Formerly in the District of Columbia. Retroceded to Virginia in 1846.

1845. [PW 147]
Plan von Washington. 1845. Meyer's Handatlas. No. 61. 12 x 14 1/2. Aus der geographischen graviranstalt des bibliographischen instituts zu Hildburghausen. Amsterdam, Paris, u. Philadelphia, [1845].
 Note.–Inset diagram of the Capitol.

1845. [PW 148]
President's house. North front. 3 1/2 x 5 1/4.
 [In Force (William Q.) Pictures of Washington. 18mo. Washington, W. Q. Force, 1845. p. 29].

1845. [PW 149]
The president's house. South view. 3 x 4 1/2.
 [In Force (William Q.) Pictures of Washington. 18mo. Washington, W. Q. Force, 1845. p. 30].

1846. [PW 150]
Map of the city of Washington established as the permanent seat of the government of the United States of America 1846. Engraved and published by D. M'Clelland, Washington. 13 1/4 x 17.
 [In Varnum (Joseph B.) The seat of government of the United States. 8vo. New York, Hunt's merchants magazine, 1848].

1846. [PW 151]
Map of the city of Washington. Established as the permanent seat of the government of the United States of America 1846. Engraved and published by D. M'Clelland. 13 x 17.
 [In Watterson (George). New guide to Washington. 18mo. Washington, R. Farnham, 1847-8. at en [sic]
 Note.–Inset "Map of the District of Columbia".

Maps and Views of District of Columbia

1847. [PW 152]
View of the Capitol.

[In Mills (Robert). Guide to the Capitol and national executive offices of the United States. 16mo. Washington, W. Greer, 1847-8. front.]

Note.–Introduction page 6, states that "A beautiful map of the city, showing the locality of every public building, churches &c. will be affixed to some of the copies of this work to meet the wishes of purchasers".

1848. [PW 153]
Capitol (East view). Drawn from nature by Aug. Köllner. Lith. by Deroy. Printed by Cattier. New York & Paris, published by Goupil, Vibert & co. Entered according to act of congress in the year 1848 by Aug. Köllner, in the clerk's office of the district court for the southern district of New York. Deposited in the Clerk's office so. district, N. Y. May 30, 1850. 8 x 11 3/4.   Art Division.

1848. [PW 154]
Capitol. East view, 1848. 3 1/2 x 6.

[In Washington, D. C. Capitol centennial committee. Centennial anniversary of the laying of the corner-stone of the National Capitol, sept. 18, 1793. 12mo. Washington, 1893. p.22].

1849. [PW 155]
City of Washington. 12 1/2 x 15 1/2.

[In Mitchell (S. A.) A new universal atlas. fol. Philadelphia, S. A. Mitchell, 1849. pl. 16].

Note.–Inset "Plan of the principal floor of the Capitol."

1849. [PW 156]
View of Washington city and Georgetown. Published and sold by Casimir Bohn. 19 x 22.

[In Bohn's hand-book of Washington. 18mo. Washington, C. Bohn, 1854. at end].

Note.–Copyright in 1849. Interesting inserted view with marginal picture of public buildings.

1850. [PW 157]
Map of the city of Washington established as the permanent seat of the government of the United States of America. 1850. Engraved and published by D. M'Clelland, Washington, 13 1/4 x 17.

[In Streeter (E. S.) The stranger's guide. 18mo. Washington, C. Alexander, 1850. at end].

Note.–Inset "Map of the District of Columbia."

MAPS AND VIEWS OF DISTRICT OF COLUMBIA

1850. [PW 158]

Map of the city of Washington, established as the permanent seat of the government of the United States of America. 1850. Engraved and published by D. M'Clelland, Washington. 13 1/4 x 17.

[In Washington, D. C. The Washington directory. 1850. Compiled by E. Waite. 12mo. Washington, C. Alexander, 1850].

Note. –Inset "Map of the District of Columbia."

1850. [PW 159]

Map of the city of Washington, D. C. James Keily, surveyor. col. fold. 30 x 42. Camden, N. J. Lloyd Van Derveer, publisher, 1850.

Note.–Inset views of Capitol, President's house, north front, National observatory, Washington monument, General post office, Patent office.

1851. [PW 160]

City of Washington. 12 1/2 x 15 1/2.

[In Mitchell (Samuel Augustus). A new universal atlas. 4to. Philadelphia, Thomas, Cowperthwait & co. 1851. no. 16].

Note.–On pl. 5 is an inset of the "District of Columbia."

1851. [PW 161]

Map of the city of Washington, D. C. established as the permanent seat of government of the United States. James Keily, surveyor. 30 x 42. Camden, N. J., L. Van Derveer, 1851.

Note.–Inset views of the Capitol, President house, statue of Washington, National observatory, Washington monument, City Hall, General Post Office, Smithsonian Institution, Treasury, Patent office.

1851. [PW 162]

A new map of the United States of America. By J. H. Young. 15 1/2 x 26.

[In Mitchell (Samuel Augustus). Mitchell's new atlas of North and South America. 4to. Philadelphia, Thomas, Cowperthwait & co. 1851. sheet 5].

Note.–Inset "District of Columbia".

1852. [PW 163]

Map of the City of Washington in the District of Columbia, established as the permanent seat of the government of the United States of America. W. J. Stone sc. Wash'n. 23 x 30 1/2.

[In maps of the District of Columbia and city of Washington, and plats of the squares and lots of the city of Washington. fol. Washington, A. B. Hamilton, 1852].

Note.–Reproduced by the U. S. Coast and Geodetic survey. No. 3063.

MAPS AND VIEWS OF DISTRICT OF COLUMBIA

1852. [PW 164]

Maps of the District of Columbia and city of Washington and plats of the squares and lots of the city of Washington. Printed in pursuance of a resolution of the Senate of the United States. 1 p. 1. 159 pl. 3 fold. maps. fol. Washington, A. B. Hamilton, 1852.

Note.–The folded maps are. 1. Territory of Columbia. By Andrew Ellicott, without name of author or date. The first topographical map of the District made about 1793, an original engraved copy of which is in this library. 2. Ellicott's plan of the city of Washington, 1792. From the engraved map of Hill. 3. Map of the city of Washington. W. J. Stone, sc. The King map of 1803? is the basis with additions and without the engraving of the capitol and president's house.

1852. [PW 165]

View of Washington. Published and sold by E. Sachse & co., Baltimore, Md. Drawn from nature and on stone by E. Sachse. Lith and print. in colors by E. Sachse & comp. Entered according to the year 1852 by E. Sachse in the clerk's office of the district court of Maryland. 18 1/2 x 28. Colored.   Art Division.

1853. [PW 166]

City of Washington. 12 1/2 x 15 1/2.

[In Mitchell (Samuel Augustus). A new universal atlas. 4to. Philadelphia, Thomas, Cowperthwait & co., 1853. sheet 16].

Note.–Inset "Plan of the principal floor of the Capitol."

1853. [PW 167]

Plat and subdivision of the Baltimore and Ohio rail road company's property, in "reservation 12" and in "square 574" in the city of Washington. Randolph Coyle. Nov. 11th, 1853. To be sold at auction nov. 23rd, 1853, at 2 o'clock, p. m. on the premises, by Jas. C. McGuire, auct. 17 x 14. [Washington], C. B. Graham, lithr., [1853].

1853. [PW 168]

Washington. 5 x 8 1/4.

[In Fanning's illustrated gazetteer of the United States. 8vo. New York, Phillips, Fanning & co. 1853. p. 379].

1853. [PW 169]

Washington. 5 x 8 1/2.

[In Phelps' hundred cities and large towns of America. 8vo. New York, 1853].

MAPS AND VIEWS OF DISTRICT OF COLUMBIA
1853. [PW 170]
Washington. 4 3/4 x 8.

[In Washington, D. C. Directories. 1853. Compiled and published by Alfred Hunter].

Note.–Inset "Plan of the Capitol". On page 48 is another plan of Washington in text followed by views of the Capitol, Senate, House of Representatives, pages 49-52

1853? [PW 171]
Plats showing the position of square south of 173 in the city of Washington and the subdivision of a portion there of into building lots. Drawn for the proprietor by R. Coyle. Scale of general plat one inch to two hundred and fifty feet of plat of lots one inch to eighty feet. 16 x 19 3/4. Richmond, Va., Ritchies & Dunnavant, [1853]?

1854. [PW 172]
Map of the city of Washington established as a permanent seat of the government of the United States of America. 1854. Engraved and published by D. M'Clelland, Washington. 13 1/4 x 17.

[In Varnum (Joseph B. jr.) The seat of government of the United States, 2d ed. 8vo. Washington, R. Farnham, 1854].

1854. [PW 173]
Map of the city of Washington in the District of Columbia, Published by Casimir Bohn, Washington. 11 1/2 x 15 1/2.

[In Bohn's hand-book of Washington. 18mo. Washington, C. Bohn, 1854].

Note:–Inset view of the Capitol.

1854. [PW 174]
Plan submitted for the alteration of the streets and av. around the Capitol consequent upon its extension, submitted by B. B. French, esq'r com'r of pub. buildings, december 6th, 1854. Wm. Forsyth, eng'r for C. P. Buildings. Scale 400 feet to one inch. 10 3/4 x 8. Baltimore, A. Hoen & Co. lith. 1854.

1854. [PW 175]
Plat & dimensions of circle on Pennsylvania avenue at intersection of Pa. avenue, New Hampshire avenue, K. street north, 23d street west, submitted by B. B. French, esq'r comm'r of pub. buildings. 18th nov'r 1854. Wm. Forsyth, eng'r for C. P. Buildings. Scale 150 ft. to one inch. 7 1/2 x 5. Baltimore, A. Hoen & co. lith. 1854.

MAPS AND VIEWS OF DISTRICT OF COLUMBIA

1854. [PW 176]
Plat of proposed carriage road, and other improvements south of the president's house agreeably to plan of A. J. Downing, for improvement of said road & grounds submitted by B. B. French, commissioner of pub. buildings. 3d. day of october, 1854. Wm. Forsyth, eng'r for C. P. Buildings. 10 3/4 x 8. Baltimore, A. Hoen & co. lith, 1834.

1854. [PW 177]
Plat triangular reservation of Pennsylvania between 20th & 21st streets west submitted by B. B. French, com'r of pub. buildings, 18th november, 1854. W. Forsyth, eng'r for the com'r of pub. buildings. Scale 40 ft. to one inch. 5 x 8 1/4. Baltimore, A. Hoen & Co. lith. 1854.

1854? [PW 178]
Glenwood cemetery, District of Columbia. Incorporated by act of congress, july 25, 1854. 14 x 13 1/2. [Washington, 1854].

1855. [PW 179]
Map of the city of Washington established as the permanent seat of the government of the United States of America, 1855. 13 1/2 x 17. Engraved and published by D. M'Clelland. Washington, D. M'Clelland, 1855.
> Note.–Inset "Map of the District of Columbia".

1855. [PW 180]
President's house. North front [&] South front. Two views.
> [In Morrison (W. M.) Morrison's stranger's guide to the city of Washington. 18mo. Washington, W. M. Morrison & co. 1855. p. 40].

1856. [PW 181]
Georgetown and the city of Washington. 11 x 14.
> [In Colton's atlas of the world. 4to. New York, J. H. Colton & co. 1855. v. 1. no. 24].
> Note.–Inset views of the Smithsonian institution, Capitol and Washington monument.

1856. [PW 182]
Plats of subdivisions of the city of Washington, D. C., compiled from the authentic records. By William Forsyth, surveyor. 3 p. 1. 62 pp. sm. fol. Washington, R. A. Waters, 1856.

Maps and Views of District of Columbia

1856. [PW 183]
View of the Capitol at Washington. W. H. Bartlett. C. J. Bentley. 5 x 7.

[In Bartlett (William Henry). The history of the United States. 8vo. New York, Virtue & Yorston, 1856? v. 2. p. 238.]

Note.–Same view also in "American scenery. By W. H. Bartlett. 1839."

1857. [PW 184]
City of Washington. Published by Charles Desilver. 12 1/2 x 15 1/2.

[In Desilver (Charles). A new universal atlas. 4to. Philadelphia, C. Desilver, 1857. sheet 16].

Note.–Inset "Plan of the principal floor of the Capitol".

1857. [PW 185]
Map of Washington city. Surveyed and published by A. Boschke. 1857. Scale 500 ft. to 1 inch. 56 x 60. New York, lith. of J. Bien, [1857].

Note.–Inset views of U. S. Treasury, National observatory, Capitol, Military asylum, National monument, President's house, Post office, Lunatic asylum, City hall, Columbia armory, Greenough's statue of Washington, U. S. arsenal.

1858. [PW 186]
Georgetown and the city of Washington.

[In Colton (W. G.) Colton's general atlas, New York, Colton & co. 1858. no. 26].

Note.–Inset views of the Smithsonian institution, Capitol and Washington monument.

1858. [PW 187]
Map of the city of Washington, established as the permanent seat of the government of the United States of America, 1858. Published by C. Bohn. 13 1/4 x 17.

[In Lanman (Charles). Bohn's hand-book of Washington 18mo. Washington, C. Bohn, 1860. at end].

1858. [PW 188]
Map of the city of Washington. 1858. 13 x 17. Washington, Cassimir Bohn, 1858.

[In Bohn (Cassimir). Handbook of Washington. 16mo. Washington, 1860. at end].

Note. –A reproduction of M' Clelland's map of 1846.

MAPS AND VIEWS OF DISTRICT OF COLUMBIA

1860. [PW 189]

President's house. 3 x 4 1/4.

[In Lanman (Charles). Bohn's hand-book of Washington. 18mo. Washington, C. Bohn, 1860. p. 31].

1861. [PW 190]

Defenses of Washington. 16 x 16.

[In United States. War department. Atlas to accompany the official records of the Union and Confederate armies. Compiled by capt. Calvin D. Cowles. 4to. Washington, government printing office, 1891-95. pl. 6].

1861. [PW 191]

G. Woolworth Colton's map of the country 500 miles around the city of Washington. Showing the seat of war in the east. 20 x 30. New York, G. W. Colton, 1861.

1861. [PW 192]

Map of the city of Washington in the District of Columbia, U. States of America. Published by Casimir Bohn, Washington. 11 x 15 1/2.

[In Bohn (Casimir). Bohn's hand-book of Washington. 18mo. Washington, C. Bohn, 1861. at end].

Note.–Inset view of the Capitol.

1861. [PW 193]

Map of the city of Washington. (District of Columbia). 6 x 7.

[In Philp's [sic] Washington described. Edited by William D. Haley. 12mo. New York, Rudd & Carleton, 1861].

1861. [PW 194]

Map of the seat of war showing the battle of july 18th, 21st & oct. 21st, 1861. 25 1/2 x 21 1/2. Washington, published by V. P. Corbett, lith. by A. Hoen & co. Balto. [1861].

[In Congressional directory for 2d sess. 37th congress. 1st ed. 8vo. Washington, 1861].

Note.–Exhibits the defences, approaches and plan of Washington.

1861. [PW 195]

Monk (Jacob). Map of the seat of war exhibiting the surrounding country, the approaches by sea & land to the Capitol of the United States, and the military posts, forts &c. col. 23 x 30. Philadelphia, J. Monk, 1861.

MAPS AND VIEWS OF DISTRICT OF COLUMBIA

1861. [PW 196]
Pocket map showing the probable theatre of the war compiled by G. A. Aschbach, c. e. 14 x 12 1/2. Philadelphia, M. H. Traubel, [1861].
Note.–Inset map of Washington city.

1861. [PW 197]
Topographical map of the District of Columbia, surveyed in the years 1856-'59 by A. Boschke. Scale 4 inches to one mile. 40 x 40. Washington, D. M'Clelland, [etc.] 1861.

1862. [PW 198]
Johnson's Georgetown and the city of Washington. 11 1/2 x 14 1/2.
[In Johnson s new illustrated family atlas. 4to. New York, Johnson & Ward, 1862. p. 34].
Note.–Inset views of the Smithsonian institution, Capitol and Washington monument.

1862. [PW 199]
Map of northeastern Virginia and vicinity of Washington. Compiled in topographical engineers office at division headquarters of general Irwin McDowell, Arlington, Jan. 1, 1862. Corrected from recent surveys and reconnaissances under direction of the bureau of topographical engineers, Aug. 1, 1862. Scale: one inch to two miles. Drawn by J. Young and W. Hesselbach. 2 sheets each. 16 1/2 x 27.
[In United States. War department. Atlas to accompany the official records of the Union and Confederate armies. Compiled by capt. Calvin D. Cowles. 4to. Washington, government printing office, 1891-95. pl. 7-8].

1862. [PW 200]
The new naval and military map of the United States. By J. Calvin Smith. 67 x 67 3/4. Philadelphia, Baker, 1862.
Note.–Inset view of Washington city.

1862. [PW 201]
Preliminary chart of Potomac river in four sheets. Sheet no. 4, from Indian head to Little Falls bridge. 1862. Scale 1/40000. 38 3/4 x 23. [Washington], 1862.
[United States. Treasury department. Coast and geodetic survey].

1862. [PW 202]
"Surveys for military defences." Map of n. eastern Virginia and vicinity of Washington, compiled in topographical engineers office at division

Maps and Views of District of Columbia

head quarters to general Irvin McDowell, Arlington, january 1, 1862. Corrected from recent surveys and reconnaissances under direction of the bureau of topographical engineers, august 1st. 1862. Drawn by J. J. Young, W. Hesselbach. Scale one inch to the mile. 52 1/2 x 51. New York, engr. on stone by J. Schedler, [1862].

[United States. War department. Corps of engineers].

1862. [PW 203]

Topographical map of the original District of Columbia and environs: showing the fortifications around the city of Washington. By E. G. Arnold. col. fold. 30 x 32. New York, G. W. Colton, 1862.

Note.–Copyright 1862 by E. G. Arnold. The position of forts is shown by red color. Gives population from 1800-1860.

1863. [PW 204]

Bird's eye view of Washington. J. Wells, N. Y. J. C. Armytage. 5 x 7 1/2.

[In Bartlett (W. H.) and Woodward (B. B.) The history of the United States. 8vo. London, Virtue & co. [1863]. v. 2. front.]

1863. [PW 205]

Map of the city of Washington (District of Columbia). W. Smith, engraver & lithographer.

[In Hannot (Victor). Street directory of Washington and Georgetown, 1863. 24mo. Washington, V. Hannot, 1863].

1863. [PW 206]

The president's house, from the river. H. W. Bartlett. W. Radclyffe. 5 x 7.

[In Bartlett (W. H.) and Woodward (B. B.) The history of the United States. 8vo. London, Virtue & Co. [1861]. v. 1. p. 601].

1863. [PW 207]

View of the Capitol completed 1863. Showing north and south wings and dome constructed under the supervision of Gen. Montgomery C. Meigs, after the design of mr. Thos. U. Waters, Philadelphia, Penna. L. C. Handy, photo., Washington. 17 x 23.

Division of Prints.

1864. [PW 208]

Colton's Georgetown and the city of Washington. 11 x 14.

[In Colton's atlas of America. 4to. New York, J. H. Colton, 1864. no. 9].

MAPS AND VIEWS OF DISTRICT OF COLUMBIA

Note.–Inset views of the Smithsonian institution, Capitol and Washington monument.

1864. [PW 209]
Johnson's Georgetown and the city of Washington. 12 1/2 x 15 1/2.

[In Johnson's new illustrated family atlas. 4to. New York, Johnson & Ward, 1864. sheet 37].

Note.–Inset views of the Smithsonian institution, Capitol and Washington monument.

1864. [PW 210]
[Washington & surrounding forts].

[In Bechler (Gustavus R.) Atlas showing battles, engagements, and important localities connected with the campaigns in Virginia. obl. 12mo. Philadelphia, [1864]. plate 1].

1865. [PW 211]
Defenses of Washington. Extract of military map of n. e. Virginia, showing forts and roads. 1865. Scale: one inch to the mile. 16 1/2 x 13.

[In United States. War department. Atlas to accompany the official records of the Union and Confederate armies. Compiled by capt. Calvin D. Cowles. 4to. Washington, government printing office, 1891-95. pl. 89].

1865. [PW 212]
Extract of military map of n. e. Virginia, showing forts and roads. Engineer bureau, war dept. 1865. 39th cong. 1st sess. Report of the chief engineer. No. 1. 16 1/2 x 23 1/2. Philadelphia, Bowen & co., [1865]. United States. War department. Corps of engineers].

1865. [PW 213]
Plan of the city of Washington. Drawn and engraved by W. H. Gamble. 11 x 13 1/2.

[In Mitchell (Samuel Augustus). Mitchell's new general atlas. 4to. Philadelphia, S. A. Mitchell, jr, 1865. no. 26].

1866. [PW 214]
The House of representatives, U. S. Capitol, Washington, D. C. Published by Casimir Bohn, Washington, D. C. Lith., by E. Sachse & co. Entered according to act of congress, A. D. 1866 by Casimir Bohn, Balto. in the clerk's office of the district court of Md. Colored. 12 x 19 1/2.

Division of Prints.

MAPS AND VIEWS OF DISTRICT OF COLUMBIA

1866. [PW 215]

Map of the city of Washington (District of Columbia). 6 1/2 x 7.

[In Washington, D. C. Directories, 1866. Compiled by Andrew Boyd. 8vo. Washington, Boyd & Waite, 1866].

1866. [PW 216]

Map of Washington city and Georgetown. Victor Hannot, publisher. A. Hoen & co. lithographers & engravers. 8 x 10.

[In Washington, D. C. Directories. Street directory. 1866. 24mo. Washington, V. Hannot, 1866].

1866. [PW 217]

Plan of the city of Washington. Drawn and engraved by W. H. Gamble. 11 x 13.

[In Mitchell (Samuel Augustus). Mitchell's new general atlas. 4to. Philadelphia, S. A. Mitchell, 1866. sheet 26].

1866. [PW 218]

Washington, D. C. 7 x 8.

[In Hall (Edward H.) Appleton's hand-book of american travel. 12mo. New York, D. Appleton & co. 1866. p. 21].

1867. [PW 219]

Hall and Elvans' subdivision of Meridian Hill, Washington county, D.C. Sept. 1867. Charles H. Bliss, surveyor. Scale: 100 feet to the inch. 35 3/4 x 29 3/4. New York, Snyder, Black & Sturn, 1867.

1867. [PW 220]

Map of the city of Washington (District of Columbia). 6 1/2 x 7.

[In Washington, D. C. Directories. 1867. Compiled by Wm. H. Boyd. 8vo. Washington, Hudson Taylor book store, 1867].

1867. [PW 221]

Plan of the city of Washington. Drawn and engraved by W. H. Gamble. 11 x 13.

[In Mitchell (Samuel Augustus). Mitchell's new general atlas. 4to. Philadelphia, S. A. Mitchell, 1867. sheet 29].

1868. [PW 222]

Johnson's Washington and Georgetown. col. fold. 13 x 17. New York, A. J. Johnson, [1868].

MAPS AND VIEWS OF DISTRICT OF COLUMBIA

1868. [PW 223]

Map of the city of Washington (District of Columbia). 6 1/2 x 7.
 [In Washington, D. C. Directories. 1868. Compiled by Wm. H. Boyd. 8vo. Washington, Hudson Taylor book store, 1868. p. 76].

1868. [PW 224]

Map of the city of Washington. 18 1/2 x 21. [Washington], W. H. &. O. H. Morrison, 1868.

1868. [PW 225]

Todd & Brown's subdivision of part of "Pleasant Plains & Mt. Pleasant", suburbs of Washington, D. C. Surveyed and divided by Wm. Forsyth, surveyor, april, 1868. 21 x 36. Washington, J. F. Gedney, 1868.

1868. [PW 226]

View of Washington city Pub. by W. H. &.O. H. Morrison. 5 1/2 x 7 1/2.
 [In Morrison's stranger's guide for Washington city. 18mo. Washington, W. H. & 0. H. Morrison, 1868].

1869. [PW 227]

Map of the city of Washington (District of Columbia). 6 1/2 x 7.
 [In Washington, D. C. Directories, 1869. Compiled by Wm. H. Boyd. 8vo. Washington, Hudson Taylor book store, 1869. p. 104].

1869. [PW 228]

View of Washington city. Publ. by J. E. Walker. Colored. 17 3/4 x 26 3/4. Baltimore, lith by E. Sachse & co. [1870].

1870. [PW 229]

Map of the city of Washington (District of Columbia). 6 1/2 x 7.
 [In Washington, D. C. Directories. 1870. Compiled by Wm. H. Boyd 8vo. Washington, Hudson Taylor book store, 1870].

1870. [PW 230]

Map of the roads in Washington county, D. C. 1870. Scale 4 inches to the mile. B. D. Carpenter, surveyor. 47 x 40. Washington, J. F. Gedney, lith [1870].

1870. [PW 231]

Map of Washington, District of Columbia. 1870. 7 x 9.
 [In Congressional directory for the 3d sess. 41st. congress. 1st. ed.

MAPS AND VIEWS OF DISTRICT OF COLUMBIA

8vo. Washington, government printing office, 1870. at end].
Note.–Same map published in all the directories to 1876 inclusive.

1870. [PW 232]
Map of Washington city, District of Columbia. 1870. 7 x 9.
[In Washington, D. C. Directories. 1871. Compiled by Wm. H. Boyd. 8vo. Washington, Hudson Taylor book store, 1871. p. 1].

1870. [PW 233]
Outlines of tracts of land within which the city of Washington was laid out. Constructed by S. R. Seibert, c. e., from data collected by dr. J. M. Toner, 1870. 45 x 66. [Washington, 1870]. Toner collection.

1870. [PW 234]
Plan of the city of Washington. Drawn and engraved by W. H. Gamble. 11 x 13.
[In Mitchell (Samuel Augustus). Mitchell's new general atlas. 4to Philadelphia, S. A. Mitchell, 1870. sheet 30].

1870. [PW 235]
Plan of the city of Washington, D. C. established as the permanent seat of the government of the United States extended to embrace its suburban towns, villages &c. and the city of Georgetown, and showing original and other valuable data not to be found on any map heretofore published. Also a diagram of the avenues showing their true courses and distances and a plan of Alexandria. By William Forsyth, 1870. 63 x 68. [Washington, 1870].

1870. [PW 236]
View of Washington city. Colored. 17 3/4 x 26 3/4. Baltimore, lith. by E. Sachse & co. [1870].

1871. [PW 237]
View of Washington city. Colored. 17 3/4 x 26 3/4. Baltimore, lith by B. Sachse & co. [1871].

1872. [PW 238]
Map of the city of Washington. Showing the subdivisions, grades and general configuration of the ground in equidistances from 5 to 5 feet altitude. Compiled with the assistance of the city sur. P. H. Donegan by A. Bastert and J. Enthoffer. Scale 1 inch-250 feet. 10 sheets each 22 x 33 1/2. fold. fol. Boston, A. Petersen & J. Enthoffer, 1872.

MAPS AND VIEWS OF DISTRICT OF COLUMBIA

1872. [PW 239]
Washington from Arlington Heights. W. Sheppard. R. Hinshelwood. 13 x 10. New York, D. Appleton & co. [1872].

1873. [PW 240]
Georgetown and the city of Washington. 11 1/2 x 15.
[In Gray (0. W.) Gray's atlas of the United States. 4to. Philadelphia, Steadman, Brown & Lyon. 1873. p. 88].
Note.–Inset views of the Smithsonian institution, Capitol and Washington momument.

1873. [PW 241]
Martenet (J. S.) & others. New topographical atlas of the state of Maryland and the District of Columbia. (etc.) 108 pp. incl. 30 maps. fol. Baltimore, Stedman, Brown & Lyon, 1873.

1873. [PW 242]
Map of the city of Washington showing the progress of buildings up to oct. 1873. Compiled by J. Enthoffer. Scale 1000 feet to the inch. 23 x 27. [Washington, 1873].
Note. –Photograph copy.

1873. [PW 243]
Plan of the city of Washington. Drawn and engraved by W. H. Gamble. 11 x 14.
[In Mitchell (Samuel Augustus). Mitchell's new general atlas. 4to. Philadelphia, S. A. Mitchell, 1873. sheet 30].

1874. [PW 244]
Map of the cities of Washington and Georgetown, D. C. Published by W. H. & 0. H. Morrison. 1874. 15 1/2 x 19 1/2.
[In Morrison's standard guide for Washington city. 18mo. Washington, W. H. & 0. H. Morrison, 1875. at end].

1874. [PW 245]
Plan for sewering the city of Washington, D. C., and at the same time purify B-street sewer and James Creek canal, and prevent floods, which are so frequent, by means of "an artificial current". By E. Bantz, m. d. Baltimore, Md. Originated 1873. Suggested 1874. 22 x 15. [Baltimore, 1874].
Note.–Manuscript plan with printed title.

MAPS AND VIEWS OF DISTRICT OF COLUMBIA

1874. [PW 246]

Real estate directory of the city of Washington, D. C. A manual for business men, [etc.] Containing a separate plat of each square in the city, on a scale of 50 feet to the inch. Prepared at the request and under the auspices of Fitch & Fox, by E. F. M. Faehtz and F. W. Pratt. 3 v. 4to. [Washington] 1874——V. 1. Squares 1-428. V.2. Squares 428-815. V.3. Squares 815-1170.

1874? [PW 247]

General plan for the extension of the U. S. capitol grounds. John Fraser, architect. 29 x 19 3/4.

    Note.–Printed from manuscript "General plan for the improvement of the U. S. capitol grounds". "By Fred Law Olmstead, july 1874. Scale 60 feet to one inch. Original plan does not contain Congressional Library or Department of Justice".

1875. [PW 248]

Maryland, Delaware and District of Columbia. By Frank A. Gray. Natural scale 1: 633,600. 15 1/2 x 26.

    [In Gray (O. W.) & son. The national atlas. 4to. Philadelphia, O. W. Gray & son, 1882. p. 63].

    Note.-Inset plan of Washington.

1875. [PW 249]

Washington. 12 x 15.

    [In Gray (O. W.) & son. The national atlas. 4to. Philadelphia. O. W. Gray & son, 1875. p. 74].

1876. [PW 250]

Bird's eye view of Washington city, D. C. Published by W. H. & O. H. Morrison. 14 x 20.

    [In Morrison's stranger's guide for Washington city. 16mo. Washington, W. H. & 0. H. Morrison, 1876].

1876. [PW 251]

Georgetown and the city of Washington. 11 x 14.

    [In Colton's general atlas of the world. 4to. New York, G. W. & C. B. Colton & co. 1876. p. 27].

    Note.–Inset views of the Smithsonian institution, Capitol and Washington monument.

MAPS AND VIEWS OF DISTRICT OF COLUMBIA
1876. [PW 252]
Map of the cities of Washington and Georgetown, D. C. Published by W. H. & 0. H. Morrison, 1876. 15 3/4 x 19 3/4.

[In United States. Congress. House of representatives. 45th cong. 2d sess. Ex. doc. 1, pt. 6. Fourth annual report of the commissioners of the District of Columbia for 1876 & 1877. 8vo. Washington, government printing office, 1877. v. 4. p. 142].

1876. [PW 253]
Map of the cities of Washington and Georgetown, D. C. Published by W. H. & 0. H. Morrison, 1876. 15 1/2 x 19 1/2.

[In Morrison's stranger's guide for Washington city. 16mo. Washington, W. H. & 0. H. Morrison, 1876. at end].

1876. [PW 254]
Map of Washington city. 5 1/2 x 7.

[In Ogden (Robert C.) Washington city and how to see it [anon.] 18mo. New York, Hurd & Houghton, 1876. p. 7].

1876. [PW 255]
Map of Washington, District of Columbia. 7 x 9.

[In Wyeth (Samuel D.) Roose's companion and guide to Washington and vicinity [anon.] 18mo. Washington, Gibson bros. 1876].

1876. [PW 256]
Maryland, Delaware and the District of Columbia. By Frank A. Gray. Natural scale 1:633.000. 15 1/2 x 26.

[In Gray (0. W.) Gray's atlas of the United States. 4to. Philadelphia, J. W. Lyon & Co. 1876. pp. 64-65].

Note.–Contains inset plan of Washington.

1876. [PW 257]
Maryland, Delaware and the District of Columbia. By Frank A. Gray. Natural scale 1: 633.600. 15 1/2 x 26.

[In Gray (0. W.) & son. The national atlas. 4to. Philadelphia, 0. W. Gray & son, 1876. pp. 64-65].

Note.–Contains inset plan of Washington.

1876. [PW 258]
New map of Maryland, Delaware and the District of Columbia. 15 x 24. Baltimore, J. F. Weishampel, jr, 1876.

MAPS AND VIEWS OF DISTRICT OF COLUMBIA

1876. [PW 259]

New railroad map of the state of Maryland, Delaware, and the District of Columbia. Compiled and drawn by Frank Arnold Gray. col. 15 x 24. Philadelphia, O. W. Gray & son, 1876.

1876. [PW 260]

Plan of the city of Washington. Drawn and engraved by W. H. Gamble. 11 x 13 1/2.

[In Mitchell (Samuel Augustus). Mitchell's new general atlas. 4to Philadelphia, S. A. Mitchell, 1876. sheet 48].

1877. [PW 261]

Map of Maryland, Delaware and the District of Columbia. 24 x 16

[In Hopkins (G. M.) Atlas of Baltimore county, Maryland. fol. Philadelphia, G.M. Hopkins, 1877].

1877. [PW 262]

Map of Washington city, District of Columbia. 1877. 7 x 9.

[In Congressional directory. 45th cong. 2d sess. Corrected to dec. 10, 1877. 1st. ed. 8vo. Washington, government printing office, 1877. at end].

Note.–Same map published in all the directories to 1878 inclusive.

1877. [PW 263]

Rand, McNally & co's indexed map of Maryland, D. C. and Delaware. 18, 6 pp. 18mo. Chicago, Rand, McNally & co. 1877.

1877-1896. [PW 264]

Potomac river (In four sheets). Date of first publication 1862-1868. Issued 1877-1896.

Sheet 1. Entrance to Piney Point. Scale 1:60,000. 23 1/4 x 29.
Sheet 2. Piney Point to Lower Ceder Point. Scale 1:60,000. 23 x 26 1/2.
Sheet 3. Lower Ceder Point to Indian Head. Scale 1:60,000. 23 x 29 1/2.
Sheet 4. Indian Head to Georgetown. Scale 1:40,000. 39 x 22 3/4.

[United States. Treasury department. Coast and Geodetic survey. Charts 388-391].

1878. [PW 265]

Georgetown and the city of Washington. 11 x 14.

[In Colton's general atlas of the world. 4to. New York, G. W. & C. B. Colton & co. 1878. no. 27].

Note.–Inset views of the Smithsonian institution, Capitol and Washington monument.

Maps and Views of District of Columbia

1878. [PW 266]
Map of Maryland, Delaware and the District of Columbia. 24 x 16.
 [In Hopkins (G. M.) Atlas of fifteen miles around Baltimore, including Anne Arundel county, Maryland. fol. Philadelphia, G. M. Hopkins, 1878. at end].

1878. [PW 267]
Map of Maryland, Delaware and the District of Columbia. 24 x 16.
 [In Hopkins (G. M.) Atlas of fifteen miles around Washington, including the county of Prince George, Maryland. fol. Philadelphia, G. M. Hopkins, 1878. at end].

1878. [PW 268]
Map of Maryland, Delaware and the District of Columbia. 24 x 16.
 [In Hopkins (G. M.) Atlas of fifteen miles around Baltimore, including Howard county, Maryland. fol. Philadelphia, G. M. Hopkins, 1878. at end].

1878. [PW 269]
Plan of the city of Washington. Drawn and engraved by W. H. Gambel. 11 x 13 1/2.
 [In Mitchell (Samuel Augustus). Mitchell's new general atlas. 4to. Philadelphia, S.A. Mitchell, 1878. p. 48].

1879. [PW 270]
Hopkins (G.M.) Atlas of fifteen miles around Washington, including the counties of Fairfax and Alexandria, Va. 77 pp. 4. incl. 49 maps. fol. Philadelphia, G. M. Hopkins, 1879.
 Note.–Plan of Washington on pp. 10-11.

1879. [PW 271]
Hopkins (G.M.) Atlas of fifteen miles around Washington, including the county of Montgomery, Maryland. 84 pp. incl. 44 maps. 3 maps at end. fol. Philadelphia, G. M. Hopkins, 1879.
 Note.–Plan of Washington on pp. 10-11.

1879. [PW 272]
Map of Maryland, Delaware and the district of Columbia. 16 x 24.
 [In Hopkins (G. M.) Atlas of fifteen miles around Washington, including the county of Montgomery, Maryland. fol. Philadelphia, G. M. Hopkins, 1879. at end].

MAPS AND VIEWS OF DISTRICT OF COLUMBIA

1879. [PW 273]
Map of Washington city, District of Coliumbia. 7 x 9.
[In Congressional directory. 45th cong. 3d sess. 2d ed. Corrected to jan. 29, 1879. 8vo. Washington, government printing office, 1879 at end].
Note.–Same map published in all the directories to 1882 inclusive.

1879. [PW 274]
Plan of the city of Washington. Drawn and engraved by W. H. Gamble. 11 x 14.
[In Mitchell (Samuel Augustus). Mitchell's new general atlas. 4to. Philadelphia, S.A. Mitchell, 1879. p. 48].

1880. [PW 275]
The city of Washington. Birds-eye view from the Potomac–looking north. Drawn by C. R. Parsons. 20 1/2 x 33. New York, Currier & Ives. [1880].

1880. [PW 276]
Plan of the city of Washington. Drawn and engraved by W. H. Gamble. 11 x 13 1/2.
[In Mitchell (Samuel Augustus). Mitchell's new general atlas. 4to. Philadelphia, Bradley & co. 1880. sheet 48].

1880. [PW 277]
Rand, McNally & co.'s indexed map of Maryland, D. C. and Delaware. 18, 6 pp. 1 fold. map. 18mo. Chicago, Rand, McNally & co., [1880].

1880. [PW 278]
Roose's companion and guide map of Washington, and vicinity. 1880. 15 1/2 x 20 1/4.
[In Roose's companion and guide to Washington and vicinity. 18mo. Washington, Gibson bros. 1882].

1880. [PW 279]
Statistical maps of Washington and the District of Columbia. 1880. Compiled by lieut. F. V. Green, to accompany the annual report of the commissioners of the District of Columbia for the year ending June 30, 1880. 13 maps. 5 diagr. fol. [Washington, 1880].

MAPS AND VIEWS OF DISTRICT OF COLUMBIA

CONTENTS

Topographical map of the District of Columbia showing the projected harbor improvement, system of main drainage and county roads as corrected to 1880.

 No. 1 Valuation of real property as determined by the assessment of 1878, and corrected to july 1st. 1879.
 No. 2. Showing the street grades.
 No. 3. Varieties of street pavements, on january 1st. 1881.
 No. 4. Lines of shade trees.
 No. 5. Location of gas lamps, maintained and lighted at the date of january 1st. 1881.
 No. 6. Lines of water mains.
 No. 7. Location of the sewers.
 No. 8. Location of the public schools.
 No. 9. Location of the stations of the Police and fire departments.
 No. 10. Location of the street railways.
 No. 11. Location of the telegraph lines.
 No. 12. Showing the schedule of street sweeping.

1880-92. [PW 280]

District of Columbia. Surveyed between 1880 and 1892. Published sept. 1894. The contour interval is 10 feet. The datum plane is 0.807 feet above half tide level of the Potomac river. Scale 1/9600. 5 sheets, each 23 x 34. Cincinnati, the Strobridge lith. co. [1894].

 [United States. Treasury department. Coast and geodetic survey. no. 3061-3066].

 Note.–Sheet no. 3165 to Washington city, not published.

1881. [PW 281]

Map of Washington city and environs. By Russell Hinman, e. c. Scale: as 1 is to 60,000. 6 x 8 1/2.

 [In Eclectic (The) atlas and hand-book of the United States. 4to. Cincinnati, Van Antwerp, Bragg & co., 1881. Map 14.]

1881. [PW 282]

Post route of the states of Pennsylvania, New Jersey Delaware and Maryland and the District of Columbia with adjacent parts of New York, [etc]. By W. L. Nicholson. The 1st ed. was issued in 1869. Drawn by C. H. Poole. Scale 6 miles to the inch. Engraved by D. M'Clelland. 4 sheets. fold. fol. [Washington, 1881].

 [United States. Post office department. Topographer's office].

1881. [PW 283]

Rand, McNally & co's indexed county and township map of Maryland and District of Columbia. 43 pp. 1 fold. map. 18mo. Chicago, Rand, McNally & co. [1881].

Maps and Views of District of Columbia

1881. [PW 284]

Roose's companion and guide map of Washington and vicinity 1881. 15 1/4 x 20.

[In Wyeth (S. D.) Roose's companion and guide to Washington and vicinity. Cheap ed. sq. 16mo. Washington, Gibson bros. 1881].

Note.–Inset "Diagram showing the divisions of the city."

1882. [PW 285]

Boyd's map of the city of Washington and suburbs, District of Columbia. 1882. 15 x 17 1/2.

[In Washington, D. C. Directories. 1884. Wm. H. Boyd, compilor. 8vo. Washington, J. B. Adams, 1884].

Note.–Same map in the Directory for 1883.

1882. [PW 286]

Capitol of the United States. Washington, D. C. Copy of Milne's celebrated photograph, giving an accurate representation of the exterior of the capitol, showing both houses in session, both flags being up. 17 3/4 x 40 3/4. Buffalo, N. Y., the Courier lith. Co., [1882].

Note.–Copyright by R. Milne, december, 1882.

1882. [PW 287]

Chart of the Potomac showing principal points and distances by A. C. Ruebsam. 3 1/4 x 5 1/4. [Washington, 1882].

1882. [PW 288]

Map of Washington and vicinity. Prepared at the office of the U. S. geological survey. 1882. 17 3/4 x 34.

[In Ward (Lester F.) Guide to the flora of Washington and vicnity. 8vo. Washington, government printing office, 1881. p.238: United States. Department of the interior. National museum. Bulletin 26].

1882. [PW 289]

Map showing the Washington city and Point Lookout railroad, and its connections. Prepared by G. W. & C. B. Colton & co. Scale of statute miles 12 to one inch. fold. 18 x 23. New York, G W. & C. B. Colton & Co. [1882].

1882. [PW 290]

Maryland, Delaware and the District of Columbia. By Frank A. Gray. Natural scale 1:633.600. 15 1/2 x 25 1/2.

MAPS AND VIEWS OF DISTRICT OF COLUMBIA

[In Gray (O. W.) & son. The national atlas. 4to. Philadelphia, O. W. Gray & son, 1882. p. 62].

Note. –Inset plan of Washington.

1882. [PW 291]

Plan of Smithsonian park. Office of public buildings & grounds, Washington, D. C. jany. 14, 1882. Forwarded to the secretary of the Smithsonian Institute with letter of this date. G. H. B. del. [anon.] Washington, 1882.

1882. [PW 292]

Plan of the city of Washington. Drawn and engraved by W. H. Gamble. 11 x 13 1/2.

[In Mitchell (Samuel Augustus). Mitchell's new general atlas. 4to. Philadelphia, Bradley & co. 1882. sheet 48].

1883. [PW 293]

District of Columbia. Joyce's process. 11 1/2 x 11 1/2.

[In Kengla (Louis A.) Contributions to the archæology of the District of Columbia. 8vo. Washington, R. A. Waters & son, 1883. at end].

1883. [PW 294]

Dodge (R. P.) Plats of the 131 squares in West Washington, (Georgetown) 1883. 1 p. l. 131 plats. fol. [Washington, 1883].

1883. [PW 295]

Johnson's Washington and Georgetown. 12 x 16.

[In Johnson's new illustrated family atlas of the world. 4to. New York, A. J. Johnson & co. 1883. sheet 48].

Note.–The frontispiece to this atlas is a view of the Capitol.

1888. [PW 296]

Map of the city of Washington. 1883. 6 3/4 x 9.

[In Congressional directory. 48th congress. 1st sess. 1st ed. Corrected to dec. 24, 1883. 8vo. Washington, government printing office, 1883 at end.

Note.–Same map published in all the directories to 1886 inclusive.

1884. [PW 297]

Boyd's map of the city of Washington and suburbs, District of Columbia, 1884. roller. 38 x 43. Washington, W. H. Boyd, 1884.

MAPS AND VIEWS OF DISTRICT OF COLUMBIA

1884. [PW 298]

[Linen tracing of squares 371 and 672 between New York avenue, North Capitol, M. and First streets; giving valuation of squares. Dec. 13, 1884. 12 x 14. n. p. 1884].

1884. [PW 299]

Map of the city of Washington. Prepared and presented by Thos. J. Fisher & co. 18 x 21 1/2. [Washington, 1884].

1884. [PW 300]

Map of the District of Columbia. 10 3/4 x 9.

[In Swinton (William) and Harrison (Henry D.) A descriptive atlas of the United States. [anon.] 4to. New York, and Chicago, Ivison, etc. 1884. p. 108].

1884. [PW 301]

Map of Washington city, District of Columbia. 6 x 7 1/2.

[In Morrison (J. M.) Illustrated dime hand-book of the National Capitol. [anon.] 18mo. Washington, C. W. Brown & co. 1884. front.]

1884. [PW 302]

Martenet's map of Maryland and District of Columbia, including a sketch of Delaware and parts of Pennsylvania, Virginia and West Virginia. By Simon J. Martenet. Scale: 3 1/2 miles in one inch. 43 3/4 x 70 1/2. Philad'a, J. L. Smith, 1884.

Note.–Inset map of Washington and Georgetown.

1884. [PW 303]

Plan of the city of Washington. Drawn and engraved by W. H. Gamble. 11 x 13 1/2.

[In Mitchell (Samuel Augustus). Mitchell's new general atlas. 4to. Philadelphia, W. M. Bradley & bro. 1884. p. 48].

1884. [PW 304]

Rand, McNally & Co.'s indexed county and township pocket map and shippers' guide of Maryland and District of Columbia. 46 pp. 1 fold. map. 18mo. Chicago, Rand, McNally & co. [1884.]

1884. [PW 305]

Vicinity of Washington. 4 1/4 x 6 1/2.

[In Harrower (Henry D.) Handy atlas of the world. [anon.] sm. 4to. New York and Chicago, Ivison, etc. 1884. p. 11].

MAPS AND VIEWS OF DISTRICT OF COLUMBIA

1885. [PW 306]
Holtzman (R. O.) Map of the city of Washington and environs. 18 1/2 x 25. [Washington, 1885].
    Note.–Copyrighted 1885, by A. G. Gedney.

1885. [PW 307]
Map of the city of Washington, D. C. Showing public buildings and places of interest. 16 1/2 x 21 1/2. New York, Hart & Von Arx, 1885.

1885. [PW 308]
Map of the city of Washington showing the location of the water mains. Chas. D. Cole, del. 30 x 39. Washington, N. Peters, 1885.
    Note.–To accompany the annual report of lieut C. McD. Townsend, U. S. A. ass't to eng'r comm'r, D. C.

1885. [PW 309]
Map of Washington city, District of Columbia. 7 1/4 x 101[sic] 1/2. [Washington, J. M. Morrison, 1885].
    Note.–Copyrighted by J. M. Morrison, 1885. Six marginal views, and nine views on reverse.

1885. [PW 310]
Martenet's map of Maryland and the District of Columbia, [etc]. By Simon J. Martenet, Baltimore, 1885. Scale 1/221760 or 3 1/2 miles in one inch. Philadelphia, J. L. Smith, 1885.

1886. [PW 311]
B. H. Warner & co's map showing a bird's eye view of the city of Washington, and suburbs. Locating the public buildings and places of interest. Prepared by A. G. Gedney. 20 x 26. Washington, B. H. Warner & co. [1886].

1886. [PW 312]
Map of the city of Washington, 1886. 6 3/4 x 9.
    [In Congressional directory. 49th. cong. 2d sess. 2d ed. Corrected to feb. 5, 1887. 8vo. Washington, government printing office, 1887. at end].

1886. [PW 313]
Map of the city of Washington, showing the varieties of street pavements on january 1st, 1886. To accompany the annual report of the commissioners of the District of Columbia, 1885. Chas. D. Cole, del. eng'r dept. D. C. 17 3/4 x 24 3/4. Washington, N. Peters, 1886.

MAPS AND VIEWS OF DISTRICT OF COLUMBIA

1886. [PW 314]
Standard guide-map of the city of Washington and environs, with marginal numerals and patent indication. Copyright and published by Arlington publishing co. Washington, 1886. Base map compiled by J. C. Lang. 18 x 22.

[In Porter (John Addison). New standard guide of the city of Washington and environs. [anon.] 12mo. Washington, Arlington publishing co. 1886].

1886. [PW 315]
Witteman (Adolph). New bond paper map of the city of Washington. 10 x 13. 1 sheet. fold. 24mo. New York, A. Witteman, 1886.

1887. [PW 316]
Hopkins (Griffith Morgan). A complete set of surveys and plats of properties in the city of Washington. title. index map. 44 pl. fol. Philadelphia, G.M. Hopkins, [1887].

1887. [PW 317]
Map of the city of Washington and surroundings showing recent subdivisions. Presented by Jas. H. Marr, agent royal insurance company of Liverpool. 20 x 26. Washington, copyrighted by A. G. Gedney, 1887.

1887. [PW 318]
Map of the District of Columbia from official records and surveys. Scale 800 feet to one inch. 69 x 49. Philadelphia, G. M. Hopkins, 1887.

1887. [PW 319]
Map of Washington, D. C. and environs, with marginal numbers and measuring tape atttachment for instantly locating points of interest within a radius of twenty miles from the capitol. Compiled from the following official sources: 1. Map of Washington made under the direction of the engineer commissioner of the District in 1887. 2. Compilation made from records in the office of the surveyor of the District, prepared in pursuance of the act of Congress approved june 4th, 1880, and from other sources by Axel Silversparre, c. e. Published by R. E. Whitman, Washington, D. C. Copyrighted 1887. 24 1/2 x 30 1/2.

[In Silversparre (Axel). Guide to Washington, D. C. and environs. 16mo. Washington, D. C. 1887.]

Maps and Views of District of Columbia

1887. [PW 320]

Map showing proximity of Carlin Springs to Washington and Alexandria. Drawn by H. W. Newby & Co. Scale: one inch-2500 feet. 15 x 21 1/2. Washington, Baxter & MacGowan, [1887].

1887. [PW 321]

Potomac river from Washington to Chesapeake bay. 1887. W.M. Dougal, sc. 8 1/2 x 13 1/2. [Washington, J. C. Entwistle, 1887].

Note.–Copyright 1887 by W. M. Dougal.

1888. [PW 322]

Estate of Samuel Bloget, Jr., one of the founders of the city of Washington, D. C. Prepared from official plan of the city of Washington, of 1870. The Blodget estate laid down from the official deed books. By Lorin Blodget, 1888. 16 1/2 x 20 1/4. [Washington 1888].

1888. [PW 323]

Map of the city of Washington. 6 3/4 x 9.

[In Congressional directory. 50th cong. 1st sess. 2d ed. Corrected to jan. 15, 1888. 8vo. Washington, government printing office, 1888. at end].

Note.–Same map published in all the directories to 1894 inclusive.

1888. [PW 324]

Map of the city of Washington, 9 x 11.

[In Standard (The) atlas and gazetteer of the world. 4to. Chicago, standard publishing co. 1888. p. 132].

Note.–Inset "District of Columbia"

1888. [PW 325]

Map of the city of Washington and vicinity. 16 1/2 x 19 1/2.

[In Keim (De B. Randolph). Washington, what to see and how to see it. 6th ed. 12mo. Washington, 1888].

Note.–This map is found in all the subsequent editions.

1888. [PW 326]

Morrison's map of the country about Washington. 20 x 25. 1 sheet fold. 18mo. Washington, J. R. D. Morrison, 1888].

1888. [PW 327]

Plat and survey and subdivision of "Washington heights" by the commissioners appointed in equity cause no. 9912. Thos. J. Fisher, Wm. P. Young, Wm. Forsyth, commissioners. 28 x 22.

MAPS AND VIEWS OF DISTRICT OF COLUMBIA

1888. [PW 328]
Roose's new map of Washington and its suburbs, 1888. Scale 3 in. to 1 mile. 15 1/2 x 20 1/2.

[In Roose's companion and guide to Washington. Cheap ed. corrected to 1888. 16mo. Washington, Gibson bros. 1888].

1888. [PW 329]
Sanborn map and publishing co. Insurance maps of Washington. title. map. 41 sheets. fol. New York, Sanborn map and publishing co. 1888.

1889. [PW 330]
Map of the city of Waashington with compliments of the Evening Star. Souvenir of march 4th, 1889. 17 x 22. Washington, D. C. Bell bros. photo-lith. [1889].

1889. [PW 331]
Maryland, Delaware and the District of Columbia. By Frank A. Gray. Natural scale 1:633.600. 15 1/2 x 25.

[In Brown (Milton R.) The continental atlas. 4to. Philadelphia, M. R. Brown, 1889. pp. 64–75].

Note.–Contains inset plan of Washington.

1889. [PW 332]
Topographical map of the District of Columbia and a portion of Virginia revised and corrected under the direction maj. W. Raymond, corps of engineers, engineer commissioner, D. C. by captain T. W. Symons, corps of engineers 1889. Authorities—Original map compiled under the direction of maj. G. J. Lydecker by capt. F. V. Greene 1884. Topographical maps of the District of Columbia made for the commissioners D. C. by the U. S. Coast and Geodetic survey. 1879- 1884. J W. Donn, assistant C. and G. survey. Military maps made by the Engineer department U. S. army, 1861-65. Boschke's map of the District of Columbia, 1861. Carpenter's assessment maps, 1882. Scale: 4 inches to one mile. Drawn by W. T. O. Bruff. 41 x 41. [New York, J. Bien & co., lith. 1889].

1889. [PW 333]
The tourist's guide to the city of Washington. Where to go and how to get there. [By J. V. F. i. e. Julia Vilett Finley. anon.] 14 1/2 x 17. [Washington, 1889].

MAPS AND VIEWS OF DISTRICT OF COLUMBIA

1890. [PW 334]
Map of Lincoln park and adjacent squares, in the city of Washington, D. C. Prepared for Bartow L. Walker by Francis R. Fava, jr. & co. civil engineers. 20 x 14 1/2. Washington, A. B. Graham, [1890].

1890. [PW 335]
The northwest extension of Massachusetts avenue, Washington, D. C., and adjacent subdivisions, according to the plan of Herman K. Viele. Drawn by John F. Fairchild. 13 1/4 x 35 3/4. Washington, Bell bros. 1890.

1890. [PW 336]
Oak View, D. C. Former suburban residence of ex. pres. Cleveland. Surveyed april 1890, by Edwin A. Greenough & co. Drawn by John T. Parsons, jr. Lots for sale by Thomas J. Fisher & co. 14 x 22. Washington, Bell bros. photo-lith. [1890].

1891. [PW 337]
Map of the city of Washington. 1891. 17 x 17.
[In Shanahan (Daniel). Shanahan's guide to Washington. sq. 18mo. Washington, W.M. Wright, 1894. front.]
Note.–Descriptive text on reverse.

1891. [PW 338]
Map of the city of Washington, District of Columbia, and adjacent portions of Maryland and Virginia, 1891. Prepared by W. Kesley Schoepf. E. H. Berry, del. 14 x 21. Washington, Bell litho. co. 1891.
Note.–Prepared for Thos. J. Fisher & co. real estate brokers.

1891. [PW 339]
Map of the District of Columbia. From official records and actual surveys. Scale 800 feet to one inch. 61 x 57. Philadelphia, G. M. Hopkins, 1891.

1891. [PW 340]
Miniature guide to Washington and public buildings. 6 3/4 x 6 3/4 [Washington]. Bell lithographing co, 1891.

1892. [PW 341]
The altograph of Washington city, or stranger's guide. An isometric view of the national capital, showing the public buildings, [etc]. By James T. Du Bois. 25 x 35. Washington, the Norris Peters Co. [1892].

Maps and Views of District of Columbia

1892. [PW 342]
Birdseye view of the national capitol including the site of the proposed world's exposition of 1892 and permanent exposition of the three Americas. 23 3/4 x 35 1/4. Baltimore, A. Hoen & co, 1888.
    Note.–Copyright 1888, by E. Kurtz Johnson, treasurer board of promotion.

1892. [PW 343]
The city of Washington. Birds-eye view from the Potomac looking north. Colored. 20 1/2 x 33. New York, Currier & Ives, [1892].

1892. [PW 344]
District of Columbia. Scale 1-4800. 48 sheets, each 14 x 14. Washington, Evans & Bartle, 1892.
    [United States. Treasury department. Coast and geodetic survey. Charts no. 3101-3164].
    Note.–Wanting sheets 3130, 3140, 3150, 3159, 3160, Nos. 3136-3138, 3145-3148, 3155-3158, comprising the city of Washington, never published. Complete in 64 sheets.

1892. [PW 345]
Hopkins (G. M.) Real estate plat of Washington, D. C. v. 1. title. index map. 43 pl. fol. Philadelphia, G. M. Hopkins, 1892.

1892. [PW 346]
Map of the District of Columbia and vicinity, showing the principal points of interest including the present condition of the defences of Washington. Compiled from the latest maps and from original surveys and reconnaissances by the engineering platoon of the engineer corps, D. C. N. G. F. L. Averill comdg. platoon. 23 1/2 x 20. Washington A. B. Graham, 1892.
    Note.–Copyright 1892 by F. L. Averill.

1892. [PW 347]
Map showing Stelwagen & Wolf (trustees') subdivision of the Schuetzen Park near Washington, Dist. of Col. Surveyed april 1892, by W. Kesley Schoepf. 18 x 18. Drawn by Edward Hamilton Berry. 18 x 18. Washington, Bell litho. co. [1892].

MAPS AND VIEWS OF DISTRICT OF COLUMBIA

1892. [PW 348]
Map of Washington, D. C. 10 x 12.
 [In Appleton (D.) & co. The handy atlas of modern geography. 4to. New York, D. Appleton & co. 1892. p. 103].

1892. [PW 349]
Map of Washington, D. C. and suburbs, showing the latest street and all new railway and street car routes. Drawn & published by the engineering platoon of the engineer corps. F. L. Averill. comdg. platoon. 1892. 20 x 20. Washington, A. B. Graham, 1892.

1892. [PW 350]
Rand, McNally & co.'s indexed county and township pocket map and shippers' guide of Maryland and District of Columbia. 54 pp. 1 fold. map. 18mo. Chicago and New York, Rand, McNally & co., [1892].

1892. [PW 351]
Washington city and its environs. Pennsylvania railroad g. a. r. edition. 15 3/4 x 19 1/2.
 [In Barksdall. (Frank N.) A hand-book of Washington [anon.] sq. 12mo. Philadelphia, Allen, Lane & Scott, 1892].

1893. [PW 352]
City of Washington. 9 x 11.
 [In Hunt & Eaton. The Columbian atlas. 4to. New York, Hunt & Eaton, 1893. p. 213].
 Note. –On page 212 is a description of the city and plans of the senate and house of representatives.

1893. [PW 353]
Map of the city of Washington, 1893. 6 1/2 x 9.
 [In Washington, D. C. Capitol centennial committee. Centennial annniversary of the laying of the corner-stone of the National Capitol, sept. 18, 1793. 12mo. Washington, 1893. at end].

1893. [PW 354]
Map of Washington, D. C. Scale: 1 mile-2 inches. 7 1/4 x 9 1/2 [Buffalo N.Y., Matthews-Northrup co. 1893].

1893. [PW 355]
Map of Washington, D. C. Rand, McNally & co's indexed atlas of the world. 19 x 26. [Chicago, Rand, McNally & co. 1893].

Maps and Views of District of Columbia

1893. [PW 356]
Maryland—District of Columbia—Virginia. Washington sheet. Surveyed in 1885-6. Edition of june, 1893. Scale 1/62500. 19 x 29. Washington, 1895.
    [United States. Interior department. Geological survey].

1893. [PW 357]
The Matthews-Northrup up-to-date map of Washington, D. C. 10 1/2 x 12. Buffalo, the Matthews-Northrup co. [1893].

1893. [PW 358]
Plan of the city of Washington. Drawn and engraved by W. H. Gamble. 9 3/4 x 12 1/2.
    [In Mitchell (Samuel Augustus). Mitchell's new general atlas. 4to. Philadelphia, A.R. Keller co. 1893. p. 48].

1893. [PW 359]
Rand, McNally & co's indexed county and township pocket map and shippers' guide of Maryland and District of Columbia. 56 pp. 1 fold. map. 18mo. Chicago and New York, Rand, McNally & co. [1893].

1893-4. [PW 360]
Real estate plat book of Washington, D. C. v. 1-3. fol. Philadelphia, G.M. Hopkins, 1893-4.
    CONTENTS.
      V. 1. North-west section.
      V. 2. North-east, south-east and south-west section.
      V. 3. West Washington, and balance of the county outside Florida ave. Boundary st.

1894. [PW 361]
Map of the city of Washington showing street lamps. To accompany the annual report of the engineer department, D. C. For the year ending june 30, 1894. Correct to june 30, 1894. 28 1/4 x 27 1/2. [Washington 1894].
    Note.–Giving width of streets and avenues and block numbers.

1894. [PW 362]
Map of the city of Washington showing the public reservations under control of office of Public buildings and grounds, prepared under the direction of colonel John M. Wilson, lieut. col. corps of engineers, U.S.A.

Maps and Views of District of Columbia

in charge of Public buildings & grounds. 1894. John Stewart, c. e. surveyor & draughtsman. To accompany the annual report upon the improvement and care of public buildings and grounds in the District of Columbia for the fiscal year ending June 30th, 1894. John M. Wilson colonel U. S. army. 16 3/4 x 23. [Washington, The Norris-Peters co. 1894].

1894. [PW 363]

Map of the city of Washington showing water mains. To accompany the annual report of the engineer department, D. C. For the year ending june 30, 1894. Mains correct to dec. 1, 1894. G. M. Lukesh, del. 27 1/2 x 27 1/4. Washington, National litho co. 1894.

Note.–This map gives block numbers, and width of streets and avenues.

1894. [PW 364]

Map of the city of Washington showing water mains. To accompany the annual report of the engineer, department, D. C. for the year ending june 30, 1894. Mains correct to dec. 1, 1894. I. M. Lukesh, del. 27 x 27. [Washington, 1894].

1894. [PW 365]

Map of Washington, D. C. 19 x 26.

[In Rand, McNally & co's new indexed atlas of the United States. [East]. Parts 5-6. fol. Chicago, Rand, McNally & co. 1894.

1894. [PW 366]

Map of Washington city, District of Columbia. 7 x 9.

[In Wyckoff (J. N.) How to know the National city, Washington, D. C. [anon.] 18mo. Washington, Anderson & co. 1894.

1894. [PW 367]

The vicinity of Washington, D. C. Scale 1/20.000 of nature. 55 x 59. Philadelphia, Griffith M. Hopkns, [1894].

1894-95. [PW 368]

Map of the city of Washington showing sewers: To accompany the annual report of the engineer department, D. C. For the year ending june 30, 1894. Correct to June 30, 1894. Posted to nov. 1st, 1895. G.M. Lukesh, del. 27 1/2 x 27 1/4. Washington, National litho. co. 1894.

Note.–This map shows block numbers, and width of streets and avenues. The manuscript corrections are by L. Cobb, jr.

MAPS AND VIEWS OF DISTRICT OF COLUMBIA

1895. [PW 369]
The city of Washington and environs. 1895. 8 1/2 x 8.

[In Congressional directory. 54th cong. 1st sess. 1st ed. Corrected to dec. 7, 1895. 8vo. Washington, government printing office, 1895. at end].

Note.–Same map published in all the directories to 1898, inclusive.

1895. [PW 370]
Map of the city of Washington showing sewers. To accompany the annual report of the engineer department, D. C. For the year ending june 30, 1895. Correct to june 30, 1895. G. M. Lukesh, del. 27 1/2 x 27 1/4. Washington, National litho. Co., 1895.

Note.–This map shows block numbers, and width of streets and avenues. It was published in 1894, but by the manuscript changes of L. Cobb, jr. has been brought up to june 30, 1895.

1895. [PW 371]
Map of Washington. Engraved for the People's publishing co. Chicago. 9 x 11 1/2.

[In Werner (The) co. The people's illustrated and descriptive family atlas of the world. 4to. Chicago, the Werner co. 1895. p. 114].

Note.–Inset "District of Columbia".

1895. [PW 372]
Map showing suburban subdivisions of the District of Columbia. To accompany the annual report of the engineer department, D. C. January, 1895. 22 x 26 3/4. [Washington, 1895].

Note.–This map contains manuscript additions showing telegraph lines of the Postal telegraph co. the Western Union Tel. co., and the telephone lines of the C. & P. Telephone co.

1895. [PW 373]
Maryland–District of Columbia–Virginia. Washington sheet. Surveyed in 1885-6. Edition of sept. 1895. Scale 1/62500. 19 x 29. Washington, 1895.

[United States. Interior Department. Geological survey].

1895. [PW 374]
Rand, McNally & co's map of the main portion of Washington. 11 x 14.

[In Garretson, Cox & co. The Columbian atlas of the world. 4to. Buffalo. Garretson, Cox & Co. 1896. p. 25].

MAPS AND VIEWS OF DISTRICT OF COLUMBIA

1895. [PW 375]

Washington. Massstab 1:39500. 8 3/4 x 5 1/2.

[In Brockhaus' konversations-lexikon. 14te aufl. 8vo. Leipzig, F. A. Brockhaus, 1895. p. 522].

1896. [PW 376]

Map of the city of Washington. Location of deaths for the year ending june 30, 1896. 28 x 28.

[In United States. Congress. House of representatives. 54th Cong. 2d sess. Doc. no. 7. Annual report of the commission of the District of Columbia for 1896. 8vo. Washington, government printing office, 1896. v. 21. map no. 1].

1896. [PW 377]

Map of the city of Washington. Showing location of fatal cases of zymotic diseases for the year ending june 30, 1896. 28 x 28.

[In United States Congress. House of representatives. 54th cong. 2d sess. Doc. no. 7. Annual report of the commission of the District of Columbia for 1896. 8vo. Washington, government printing office, 1896. v. 21. map no. 2].

1896. [PW 378]

Map of the city of Washington. Showing location of fatal cases of diphtheria and scarlet fever; also number of cases thereof reported to the health department during the year ending june 30, 1896. 28 x 28.

[In United States Congress. House of representatives. 54th cong. 2d sess. Doc. no. 7. Annual report of the commissioners of the District of Columbia for 1896. 8vo. Washington, government printing office, 1896. v. 21. map no. 3].

1896. [PW 379]

Map of the city of Washington showing location of fatal cases of diarrhœal diseases for the year ending june 30, 1896. 28 x 28.

[In United States Congress. House of representatives. 54th cong. 2d sess. Doc. no. 7. Annual report of the commissioners of the District of Columbia for 1896. 8vo. Washington government printing office, 1896. v. 21. map no. 4].

1896. [PW 380]

Map of the city of Washington. Showing location of fatal cases of consumption for the year ending June 30, 1896. 28 x 28.

[In United States Congress. House of representatives. 54th cong. 2d sess. Doc. no. 7. Annual report of the commissioners of the District of Columbia for 1896. 8vo. Washington, government printing office, 1896. v. 21. map no. 5].

MAPS AND VIEWS OF DISTRICT OF COLUMBIA

1896. [PW 381]
Map of the city of Washington. Showing location of fatal cases of acute lung diseases for the year ending june 30, 1896. 28 x 28.

[In United States Congress. House of representatives. 54th cong. 2d sess. Doc. no. 7. Annual report of the Commissioners of the District of Columbia for 1896. 8vo. Washington, government printing office, 1896. v. 21. map no. 6].

1896. [PW 382]
Map of portions of Maryland, Virginia and District of Columbia showing distribution of the Potomac formation in part overlain by Columbia and Lafayette formation. From data furnished by N. H. Darton. 8 miles=one inch. 1896. 19 x 7 1/2.

[United States. Department of the interior. Geological survey. Bulletin no. 145].

Note.–To accompany "The Potomac formation in Virginia. By Wm. Morris Fontaine."

1896. [PW 383]
Map of Washington. 9 x 11 1/2.

[In Fort Dearborn publishing co. The national standard family and business atlas of the world. 4to. Chicago, the Fort Dearborn publishing co. 1896. pp. 206-207].

1896. [PW 384]
Map of Washington. 9 x 11 1/2.

[In Waite (Jno. F.) publishing co. The new international office and family atlas of the world. 4to. Chicago, J. F. Waite publ. 1896. p. 94].

Note.–Inset "District of Columbia."

1896. [PW 385]
Official map of Washington. Prepared by the committee of '96. Fifteenth international Christian endeavor convention, july 8-13, 1896. 18 x 22 1/2. Washington, D. C. The Norris-Peters Co. [1896].

1896. [PW 386]
Part of the District of Columbia. June, 1896. Compiled and drawn at the office of the engineer commissioner, District of Columbia. Scale 1:12000. 38 1/2 x 54 1/2. Washington, the Norris Peters Co. [1896].

MAPS AND VIEWS OF DISTRICT OF COLUMBIA

1896. [PW 387]
Rand, McNally & co's map of the main portion of Washington, D.C. 11 x 14.

[In Rand, McNally & co. New pictorial atlas of the world. 4to. Chicago, Rand, McNally & co. 1896. p. 58].

1896. [PW 388]
Real estate plat book of Washington. Supplement. v. 3. Comprising the first suburban section of the plan of the extension of permanent system of highways. title. index sheets. 12 pl. fol. Philadelphia, Griffith M. Hopkins, 1896.

1896. [PW 389]
Robert's road map of the District of Columbia and adjoining portions of Maryland and Virginia. 16 1/2 x 22 1/2. [Washington, W. F. Roberts, 1896.]

1897. [PW 390]
Jarvis' map of Washington. 6 1/2 x 9. [Washington], J. F. Jarvis, 1897.

1897. [PW 391]
League of American wheelmen. Road book of Maryland containing all the through and sub-routes of the state of Maryland, and the principal runs and connections of lower Pennsylvania, New Jersey, District of Columbia, Virginia, West Virginia, North Carolina, and all points of importance throughout this section of the middle Atlantic and upper southern states. Based on the extended and personal surveys of Robinson C. Watters. XXX, 230 pp. 3 maps at end. 16mo. Baltimore, J. C. Dulany co. [1897].

Note.–Copyrighted by Conway W. Sams, chief consul Maryland division, L. A. W.

1897. [PW 392]
Map of the city of Washington. Sewers & water courses. 7 1/2 x 10.

[In United States. Congress. House of representatives. 55th cong. 2d sess. Doc. no. 7. Report of the commissioners of the District of Columbia for 1897. 8vo. Washington, government printing office, 1897. v. 2. p. 103. no. 3].

MAPS AND VIEWS OF DISTRICT OF COLUMBIA

1897. [PW 393]
Map of the city of Washington showing conduits of the electric lighting, telegraph, & telephone companies. Correct to sept. 1897. 28 x 28.

[In United States. Congress. House of representatives. 55th cong. 2d sess. Doc. no. 7. Report of the commissioners of the District of Columbia for 1897. 8vo. Washington, government printing office, 1897. v. 2. p. 226. map 3].

1897. [PW 394]
Map of the city of Washington. Showing location of fatal cases of zymotic diseases for the year ending june 30, 1897. 28 x 28.

[In United States. Congress. House of representatives. 55th cong. 2d sess. Doc. no. 7. Report of the commissioners of the District of Columbia for 1897. 8vo. Washington, government printing office, 1897. v. 2. map no. 1].

1897. [PW 395]
Map of the city of Washington. Showing location of fatal cases of diphtheria and scarlet fever; also number of cases thereof reported to the health department during the year ending june 30, 1897. 28 x 28.

[In United States. Congress. House of representatives. 55th cong. 2d sess. Doc. no. 7. Report of the commissioners of the District of Columbia for 1897. 8vo. Washington, government printing office, 1897. v. 2. map no. 2].

1897. [PW 396]
Map of the city of Washington. Showing location of fatal cases of diarrhœal diseases for the year ending june 30, 1897. 28 x 28.

[In United States. Congress. House of representatives. 55th cong. 2d sess. Doc. no. 7. Report of the commissioners of the District of Columbia for 1897. 8vo. Washington, government printing office, 1897. v. 2. map 3].

1897. [PW 397]
Map of the city of Washington. Showing location of fatal cases of acute lung diseases for the year ending june 30, 1897. 28 x 28.

[In United States. Congress. House of representatives. 55th cong. 2d sess. Doc. no. 7. Report of the commissioners of the District of Colurnbia for 1897. 8vo. Washington, government printing office, 1897. v. 2. map no. 4].

1897. [PW 398]
Map of the city of Washington. Showing location of fatal cases of consumption for the year ending june 30, 1897. 28 x 28.

[In United States. Congress. House of representatives. 55th cong. 2d sess. Doc. no. 7. Report of the commissioners of the District of Columbia for 1897. 8vo. Washington, government printing office, 1897. v. 2. map no. 5].

Maps and Views of District of Columbia

1897. [PW 399]

Map of Washington, D. C. 19 x 25 1/2.

[In Rand, McNally & co's enlarged business atlas and shippers' guide. fol. Chicago, Rand, McNally & co. 1897. pp. 90-91].

Note.–First copyrighted in 1895.

1897. [PW 400]

Map showing limits of low, middle and high service distribution in the District of Columbia, 1897. 15 x 11 1/2.

[In United States. Congress. House of representatives. 55th cong. 2d sess. Doc. no. 7. Report of the commissioners of the District of Columbia for 1897. 8vo. Washington, government printing office, 1897. v. 2. p. 195. no. 2].

1897. [PW 401]

Maryland and Delaware. Scale 16 english statute miles to one inch. 10 1/2 x 15.

[In Century (The) atlas of the world. 4to. New York, the century co. 1897. no. 33].

Note.–Inset "District of Columbia coextensive with Washington." Scale, 4 miles to one inch.

1897. [PW 402]

Plan der bundeshauptstadt Washington. Massstab 1:60 000. 4 1/2 x 5.

[In Meyers konversations-lexikon. 5te aufl. 8vo. Leipzig und Wien, bibliographisches institut, 1897. v. 17. p. 536].

1897-99. [PW 403]

Permanent system of highways, District of Columbia. Three sections. Scale 600 feet to one inch. 46 1/2 x 27, 46 1/4 x 28. Washington, engineer commissioner, 1897-99.

Note.–Section I. was published in 1899, section 2, in 1898, section 3, in 1897. Section I has the title "Highway extension plan of the District of Columbia." Section 2, has the imprint of A. Hoen & co., Baltimore.

1897. [PW 404]

Rand, McNally & co's indexed county and township pocket map and shippers' guide of Maryland and District of Columbia. 56 pp. 1 fold. map. 18mo. Chicago and New York, Rand, McNally & co. [1897].

1897. [PW 405]

Road book of the District of Columbia division of league of american wheelmen, containing also some of the principal routes in Maryland and Virginia, [etc.] 1st ed. 3 p. 1. 76 pp. 3 fold. maps. obl. 12mo. [Washington, G. E. Williams, 1897].

Maps and Views of District of Columbia

1898. [PW 406]

Map of the city of Washington. 28 1/4 x 28. Washington, Norris Peters Co. [1898].

Note.–This map gives block numbers, and the width of streets and avenues. It was published by direction of District commissioners for use as a base map

1898. [PW 407]

The city of Washington and environs. 1898. 14 x 14.

[In United States Congress. House of representatives. 55th cong. 2d [sic] sess. Doc. no. 7. Report of the commissioners of the District of Columbia for 1898. 8vo. Washington, government printing office, 1898. v. 1. p. 461].

Note.–Showing the various methods of street cleaning.

1898. [PW 408]

Map of the city of Washington. Police district area. 72 9/10 sq. miles. Arranged by Richard Sylvester. 7 1/2 x 10.

[In United States. Congress. House of representatives. 55th cong. 3d sess. Doc. no. 7. Report of the commissioners of the District of Columbia for 1898. 8vo. Washington, government printing office, 1898. v. 1. p. 137].

1898. [PW 409]

Map of the city of Washington. Showing location of fatal cases of acute lung diseases for the year ended june 30, 1898. 28 x 28.

[In United States. Congress. House of representatives. 55th cong. 3d sess. Doc. no. 7. Report of the commissioners of the District of Columbia for 1898. 8vo. Washington, government printing office, 1898. v. 2. map no. 4].

1898. [PW 410]

Map of the city of Washington. Showing location of fatal cases of consumption for the year ended june 30, 1898. 28 x 28.

[In United States. Congress. House of representatives. 55th cong. 3d sess. Doc. no. 7. Report of the commissioners of the District of Columbia for 1898. 8vo. Washington, government printing office, 1898. v. 2. map no. 5].

1898. [PW 411]

Map of the city of Washington. Showing location of fatal cases of zymotic diseases for the year ended june 30, 1898. 28 x 28.

[In United States. Congress. House of representatives. 55th cong. 3d sess. Doc. no. 7. Report of the commissioners of the District of Columbia for 1898. 8vo. Washington, government printing office, 1898. v. 2. map no. 1].

MAPS AND VIEWS OF DISTRICT OF COLUMBIA

1898. [PW 412]

Map of the city of Washington. Showing location of fatal cases of diphtheria and scarlet fever; also number of cases thereof reported to the health department during the year ended june 30, 1898. 28 x 28.

[In United States. Congress. House of representatives. 55th cong. 3d sess. Doc. no. 7. Report of the commissioners of the District of Columbia for 1898. 8vo. Washington, government printing office, 1898. v. 2. map no. 2].

1898. [PW 413]

Map of the city of Washington. Showing location of fatal cases of diarrhœal diseases for the year ended june 30, 1898. 28 x 28.

[In United States. Congress. House of representatives. 55th cong. 3d sess. Doc. no. 7. Report of the commissioners of the District of Columbia for 1898. 8vo. Washington, government printing office, 1898. v. 2. map no. 3].

1898. [PW 414]

Map of the District of Columbia, showing the boundary between the city of Washington and the county. To accompany the annual report of the Engineer department, D. C. January, 1898. 22 1/4 x 26 1/2.

[In United States. Congress. House of representatives. 55th cong. 2d sess. Doc. no. 7. Report of the commissioners of the District of Columbia for 1897. 8vo. Washington, government printing office, 1897. v. 2. p. 292. map 5].

1898. [PW 415]

Map of the city of Washington. Showing principal supply mains also the area supplied by pumping, the areas supplied by 48, 36, 30 and 12 in: mains, and areas where the pressure is 20 lbs. and under. 42 1/2 x 28.

[In United States. Congress. House of representatives. 55th cong. 3d sess. Doc. no. 7. Report of the commissioners of the District of Columbia for 1898. 8vo. Washington, government printing office, 1898. v. 2. p. 139].

1898. [PW 416]

Map of the city of Washington, showing the main overhead lines inside of the fire limits. 28 x 28.

[In United States. Congress. House of representatives. 55th cong. 3d sess Doc. no. 7. Report of the commissioners of the District of Columbia for 1898. 8vo. Washington, government printing office, 1898. v. 2. p. 178].

1898. [PW 417]

The Matthews-Northrup handy-map of Washington, D. C. 4 1/2 x 6 3/4.

[In Matthews-Northrup co. Complete handy atlas of the world. 12mo. Chicago, etc. Orange Judd co. 1898. p. 54].

Maps and Views of District of Columbia

1898. [PW 418]

Rand, McNally & co's indexed county and township pocket map and shippers' guide of Maryland and District of Columbia. 56 pp. 1 fold. map. 18mo. Chicago and New York, Rand, McNally & co. [1898].

1898. [PW 419]

Washington, D. C. 19 x 25 1/2.

[In Rand, McNally & co's indexed atlas of the world. fol. Chicago and New York, Rand, McNally & co. 1898. pp. 282–83].

Note.–Known as "Business atlas map." First copyrighted in 1895.

1899. [PW 420]

Chevy Chase. Section 2. Thos. J. Fisher & Co. sole agent. 24 x 19. Washington, the Norris Peters Co. photo. [1899].

1899. [PW 421]

Cliffbourne. Lots for sale by Thomas J. Fisher & Co. 13 x 22. Washington, the Norris Peters Co. photo. lith [1899].

1899. [PW 422]

Map of the city of Washington. Chas. D. Cole, draftsman. 32 x 27 1/2. [Washington, District Commissioners, 1899].

Note. –This map is a base upon which the water department maps are laid down.

1899. [PW 423]

Map of the District of Columbia. Prepared especially for and presented with compliments of Thos. J. Fisher & Co. 1899. 21 x 23. Washington, A. B. Graham, photo. lith. [1899].

1899. [PW 424]

Map of Washington. 9 x 11 1/2.

[In Cram's bankers' and brokers' railroad atlas. fol. New York, Chicago C. F. Cram, 1899. p. 483].

1899. [PW 425]

Plat compiled from official records for Thomas J. Fisher & Co., real estate brokers. 36 x 24. [Washington, 1899].

Note. –14th street extended between Florida ave and Park st., Whitney avenue, etc.

Maps and Views of District of Columbia

1899. [PW 426]
Rand, McNally & co's map of the main portion of Washington, D. C. 12 1/2 x 10 3/4.

[In Rand, McNally & co's universal atlas of the world. 4to. Chicago, Rand, McNally & co. 1899. p. 25].

Note–First copyrighted in 1895.

1899. [PW 427]
Rand, McNally & Co's map of the main portion of Washington, D. C. 12 1/2 x 10 3/4.

[In Chicago (The) chronicle's unrivaled atlas of the world. 4to. Chicago, for the Chicago chronicle by Rand, McNally & co. 1899. p. 25].

Note.–Copyright 1895 by Rand, McNally & co.

1899. [PW 428]
Rand, McNally & Co's map of the main portion of Washington, D. C. 12 1/2 x 10 3/4

[In Philadelphia public ledger's unrivaled atlas of the world. 4to. Philadelphia, for the public ledger, 1899. p. 59].

Note.–Copyright 1895 by Rand, McNally & co.

1899. [PW 429]
Soldier's Home grounds. Thomas J. Fisher & co. 29 3/4 x 9 1/2. Washington, A. B. Graham, photo. lith 1899.

1899. [PW 430]
Washington, D. C. 19 x 25 1/2.

[In Rand, McNally & co's enlarged business atlas and shippers' guide. 29th ed. fol. Chicago, Rand, McNally & Co. 1899. pp. 102-103].

Note.–First copyrighted in 1895.

1899. [PW 431]
Washington, D. C. 19 x 25 1/2.

[In Rand, McNally & co's new standard atlas of the world. fol. Chicago and New York, Rand, McNally & Co. 1899. pp. 324-325].

Note.–First copyrighted in 1895.

1900. [PW 432]
Map of the city of Washington, showing water mains and fire hydrants. Jan. 15th, 1900. Prepared from records of the water dep't, D. C. Chas. D. Cole, draftsman. 33 x 27 1/4. [Washington, Norris-Peters Co. 1900].

Maps and Views of District of Columbia

PROPERTY MAPS MOSTLY MANUSCRIPT, ETC. WITHOUT DATES ARRANGED UNDER SUBJECTS.

Blodget (Samuel). [PW 433]
    Map of that part of the city of Washington on which is situated a mansion-house belonging to Samuel Blodget. ms. 13 x 18.

Burns (David). [PW 434]
    Map of that part of the city of Washington, on which is situated a house and graveyard belonging to David Burns; at present occupied by James Burns. ms. 13 x 18.

Carroll (Daniel). [PW 435]
    Plan of that part of the city of Washington; shewing the situation of the buildings belonging to mr. Danl. Carroll, of Duddington. ms. 15 x 18 1/4.

Carroll (Daniel) & others. [PW 436]
    Plan of part of the city of Washington on which is exhibited the division of lots made under a commission from the high court of chancery of the state of Maryland and directed to Danl. Carroll of Duddington, Thomas Peter and Nicholas King. ms. 16 1/2 x 20 1/2.

Clinton (Thomas G.) [PW 437]
    Plan placing the current channel of the Potomac permanently along the wharves of Washington, D. C. Respectfully submitted by Thos. G. Clinton. 71 x 48.
    Note. –Manuscript plan.

Davidson (James). [PW 438]
    Map of that part of the city of Washington on which is situated the house and grave-yard belonging to the heirs of John Davidson. Ms. 18 x 15.

Davidson (Samuel). [PW 439]
    Plan of square 183 in the city of Washington on which is shewn the situation of a log dwelling house belonging to Samuel Davidson, original proprietor of the square. Ms. 7 1/2 x 11.

Fenwick (Mrs.———) [PW 440]
    Map of that part of the city on which mrs. Fenwick's house stands. ms. 13 x 14.

Maps and Views of District of Columbia

Lingan (James M.) [PW 441]
    Map of that part of the city of Washington on which is situated a mansion-house belonging to James M. Lingan. ms. 13 x 18.

Lynch and Sands. [PW 442]
    Map of that part of the city of Washington on which messers Lynch and Sands mansion-house stands. ms. 13 x 18.

Mills (Robert). [PW 443]
    President's house. North front. Robt. Mills, archt. One view among eight relating to buildings in Washington on one sheet. Without date. In Art Division.

Peter (Robert). [PW 444]
    Map of that part of Washington on which is situated a house belonging to Robert Peter. ms.

Peter (Robert). [PW 445]
    A plan, exhibiting the squares on which Robert Peter's building stood on that tract of land called Mexico, within the city of Washington. ms. 14 1/2 x 18.
    Plan of the squares of the eastern extreme of the city of W. [anon.] ms. 13 x 15.

Prout (Mrs.———). [PW 446]
    Map of that part of the city on which mrs. Prout's house stands. ms. 13 x 18.

Tiber creek. [PW 447]
    [Map of Tibor (sic) creek and the Mall]. ms. 11 1/2 x 23.

Walker (George). [PW 448]
    Map of that part of the city of Washington, on which is situated the mansion-house & grave-yard belonging to mr. Geo. Walker. ms. 13 x 18.

Wheler (Widow). [PW 449]
    Plan of part of the city of Washington, in the vicinity of upper Eastern Branch ferry; shewing the situation of the buildings & grave-yards, belonging to the widow Wheler. ms. 15 x 19 1/2.

Young (Abraham). [PW 450]
    Map of that part of the city of Washington on which is situated a mansion-house and grave-yard belonging to Abraham Young. ms. 13 x 18.

MAPS AND VIEWS OF DISTRICT OF COLUMBIA

Young (Notley). [PW 451]
    Map of that part of the city of Washington, shewing the situation of the mansion-house, grave-yard & buildings belonging to mr. Notley Young, original proprietor of that part of the city. Scale 100 ft. pr. inch. ms. 13 x 33.

Young (Widow). [PW 452]
    Map of that part of the city of Washington on which is situated the mansion-house and grave-yard of the widow Young. ms. 12 1/2 x 14 1/4.

Young's (Mr.) mill. [PW 453]
    Map of that part of the city of Washington on which mr. Young's mill stands. ms. 19 x 27.

o